UNSAFE THINKING

UNSAFE THINKING

How to Be Nimble and Bold
When You Need It Most

JONAH SACHS

Da Capo

LIFE
LONG

Da Capo Lifelong Books
Hachette Book Group
1290 Avenue of the Americas, New York, NY 10104
www.dacapopress.com
@DaCapoPress

Printed in the United States of America
First Edition: April 2018

Published by Da Capo Lifelong Books, an imprint of Perseus Books, LLC, a subsidiary of Hachette Book Group, Inc. The Da Capo Lifelong Books name and logo is a trademark of the Hachette Book Group.

The Hachette Speakers Bureau provides a wide range of authors for speaking events. To find out more, go to www.hachettespeakersbureau.com or call (866) 376-6591.

The publisher is not responsible for websites (or their content) that are not owned by the publisher.

Print book interior design by Jeff Williams

Library of Congress Cataloging-in-Publication Data

Names: Sachs, Jonah, author.
Title: Unsafe thinking : how to be nimble and bold when you need it most / by Jonah Sachs.
Description: First edition. | Boston : Da Capo Lifelong Books, 2018. | Includes bibliographical references and index.
Identifiers: LCCN 2017048102| ISBN 9780738220147 (hardcover) | ISBN 9780738220154 (ebook)
Subjects: LCSH: Executive ability. | Success in business.
Classification: LCC HD38.2 .S23 2018 | DDC 658.4/09—dc23
LC record available at https://lccn.loc.gov/2017048102

ISBNs: 978-0-7382-2014-7 (hardcover); 978-0-7382-2015-4 (ebook)

LSC-C

10 9 8 7 6 5 4 3 2 1

CONTENTS

Part 3: Learning

Part 4: Flexibility

Part 5: Morality

Part 6: Leadership

For Chelsea

PROLOGUE:
THE DANGERS OF SAFETY

The press conference ended in a burst of choreographed and festive chaos. Two goats stood nervously on the stage next to a few caged hedgehogs as confetti fell from the ceiling.

The occasion was the announcement of a new name for a minor-league baseball team that was about to move into a brand-new $56 million stadium in downtown Hartford, Connecticut. The team, which was supposed to reinject pride into a long-suffering community, would be known as the Yard Goats. The Hedgehogs had been a close runner-up.

Some in the crowd responded with a forced and tepid cheer. Others stood silently, perplexed.

Reaction was swift and merciless. "Worst thing I ever heard of," snarled an eighty-seven-year-old man who had been a dedicated fan of the team, formerly known as the Rock Cats. He vowed never to watch another game. Twitter lit up with derision. Some suggested the name was an affront to the city's growing population of Jamaicans, many of whom raised and ate goats. Some 6,000 names, submitted to a crowd-sourced contest, had been considered. Somehow this one had risen to the top. "Yard Goats?" the fans demanded. "That's the best you could do?"

To Jason Klein everything was going exactly according to plan. The anger and rejection that greeted his creations never felt good exactly, but by now he knew this type of response signaled that he had struck a nerve. The people of El Paso, Texas, had been angered when he named their team the Chihuahuas. The people of Lehigh, Pennsylvania, and

Richmond, Virginia, had received the Iron Pigs and the Flying Squir-rels with the same ire. Under pressure from fans, Klein's clients had of-ten considered abandoning the brands he created for them and ending their relationship with his firm. But within a year, in all these cities and dozens more where his firm's touch had been felt, sales of team mer-chandise had shot off the charts, setting minor-league sales records. People bought hats adorned with a slab of bacon, not just in Lehigh but across the country. They ate nachos out of dog bowls at the Chihuahuas' games and then proudly displayed the empties on their mantels at home. These franchises generated buzz, and profits, that teams with respectable names, like the San Jose Giants, simply couldn't keep up with.

"If you're feeling nervous, that's a good spot to be in," Klein says. "Stuff people expect gets forgotten quickly. On their mental computers they drag it right to the 'I've seen it before folder.' And then it's game over."

For many minor-league franchises, game over was becoming a real possibility. With the proliferation of competing entertainment options available in smaller towns and a decline in baseball interest, owners had been looking instinctively to the still-thriving major leagues to figure out how to compete. But Klein and his firm Brandiose turned that ob-vious approach on its head. Minor-league teams, he reasoned, provide local family entertainment. The minors, he evangelized, can either be second-rate sport or first-rate spectacle. This assertion may offend die-hard fans, but Klein's work has had enormous influence in the industry. Announcing their name change away from the Braves, the president of the newly minted Richmond Flying Squirrels stepped up to the micro-phone and said, "I'd like to address the media for a moment. People are questioning whether we're in the baseball business or the circus busi-ness. Let me be really clear, we're in the circus business."

The names Klein chooses to create spectacle aren't as random as they might appear. The Yard Goats makes a very logical kind of sense for Hartford. You just have to change your perspective a bit to see it. The moniker refers to the small cars that pulled larger trains through the railyards decades ago. The scrappy sound of the name invokes a spirit of stubbornness and irreverence, traits that Hartford residents enthusi-astically cite to describe their city's character. Because the name sounds so wrong at first, but so right once you stop to think about it, the Yard Goats would soon become an inside joke that only Hartforders would get. And that's why the name ultimately worked.

Klein could have made the citizens of Hartford and his client momentarily happy with a safer team name like the Huckleberries, the choice of *Hartford Courant* readers, in honor of Mark Twain's history in the city. He would have gotten the high fives and the approval we're all after. And his firm would almost certainly be struggling in a sea of sameness now. Instead, he has found a way to overcome his natural bias to seek safety and approval. In doing so he's sparked a revolution of growth in what was becoming a stagnant industry.

Klein is an unsafe thinker. He chose not to freeze in the face of the rapid changes tearing minor-league baseball apart. Rather, he saw the turmoil as an opportunity. He approached the problem with a spirit of courage and playfulness that he knew industry experts wouldn't accept and would thus put his reputation at risk. And in doing so, he discovered a kind of genius in the bizarre and counterintuitive form of Iron Pigs, Flying Squirrels, and Yard Goats.

But why are there so few Jason Kleins out there? Why do a small number of individuals and organizations consistently thrive in conditions of rapid change while so many more attain a certain level of success only to get stuck in a rut? Why do so few of us take a flexible, nimble approach to unfamiliar challenges while the rest of us hold on to outdated or incremental solutions? Why, when the need for bold, intelligent risks becomes obvious, do we instinctively reach for safety and stability?

In 2013, when I first heard about Klein, these questions were becoming urgent to the point of obsession for me. The advertising company I'd founded was on the verge of collapse. Our problem came down to our fixation on a so-called creative process that was crushing our creativity. What's worse, it was all my fault.

I had started Free Range back in 1999 straight out of college, when I was twenty-four years old, because I didn't think I could work well in a traditional corporate structure. I had trouble following rules and predetermined processes, and I figured that if I worked in a bureaucratic company, I'd inevitably get fired. I was determined that Free Range would allow creative teams to experiment freely, entertaining even the most outlandish ideas. Our early successes bore the concept out. We made a four-minute online cartoon about the problems with factory farming that starred trenchcoated animals. *The Meatrix* reached 30 million viewers long before most people had even heard of internet video, making them laugh at and then act on an issue nobody had been talking about.

Another film, *The Story of Stuff*, broke all the rules of online marketing, clocking in at twenty minutes, trying to convince people that shopping just isn't the point of life. Played by teachers in thousands of classrooms across the globe, it wound up with even more viewers than *The Meatrix*. As these wacky wins mounted, our name became synonymous with offbeat, internet-savvy ways of changing the world. We loved where we were.

But as our firm grew from two to forty people, so did the pressure I felt to make our successes repeatable and predictable. To serve our growing list of clients, I made what seemed like a mature decision: to fashion a rigorous process for us to follow. And thus I began to morph from the twenty-four-year-old who hated rules into a thirty-eight-year-old seeking safety in them. I subscribed to management magazines, hired consultants, and instituted standard operating procedures, detailing a step-by-step path to creative success. I even wrote a book about our storytelling methodology, leading to a constant stream of people seeking my expert advice. Deep down, though, I always felt uncomfortable dispensing this wisdom. I suspected I was still a student of the concepts I was now confidently teaching. I answered questions quickly and decisively, fearing exposure of my inner uncertainty.

The methods that I developed provided some needed structure to our projects. But the process I'd imposed was also starting to tear my team apart. Once joyful collaborators were now squabbling about who understood and applied our methodology most effectively. People started complaining that they felt boxed in, and I could tell that they weren't pushing themselves the way they once had. Our work was getting staid. I was as unhappy as everyone else. Perhaps most unsettling of all, up-and-coming young creatives whom I had spent months recruiting started abruptly quitting after only a short time onboard. Most told me they wanted more creative freedom.

Just a few years earlier, I had confidently believed that the social and environmental campaigns we were working on were helping to change the world. Now I seemed unable to change even my tiny corner of it. I was afraid to do away with a process that was effectively growing our business, but I could also see that we were in danger of falling apart before long.

In my gut, I knew that if I stuck to the status quo, the supposedly safer route to success, we would in fact be on the road to failure. But as the pressure to produce mounted, the status quo exerted a magnetic pull on my psyche. The tension was becoming extremely painful. As a self-identified "creative" I was used to improvising my way out of dilemmas. But now when I looked within for answers, I came up empty.

So I began a search for bold innovators: people whose work I admired, who had taken great risks and defied convention to produce beautiful and valuable things. I wanted to know whether they were simply naturally inclined to take such creative risks or if there were ways to learn to practice unsafe thinking. I made a list of the most exciting unsafe thinkers and started reaching out to them. Many were eager to share their insights. I told them I wanted to hear about what enabled them both to break free from the status quo and to bring others along with them. How did they overcome the anxiety of pursuing unconventional ideas? Or did they simply not feel the same kind of anxiety about taking those risks that I did? How did they stop themselves from reflexively falling back on established rules? And, perhaps most importantly, could they share the techniques that allowed them to keep operating in the unsafe zone?

I had more than a hundred conversations. In addition to talking with Jason Klein, I met two economists who upended conventional wisdom (and even conventional morality) by challenging the "teach a man to fish" adage and simply giving money away to people in Africa, $1,000 at a time. Their model put them under fire from their colleagues and the development world, but pressing on, they quickly became one of the top-rated charities on the planet. Recently they received a grant for $25 million to scale their work. The pioneers at GiveDirectly showed me how the right mix of insight and scientific rigor can challenge and ultimately reverse unquestioned cultural intuition.

I spent time with an Australian doctor who infected himself with a previously incurable disease he was sure he could cure, even though no one else believed him. Barry Marshall's desperate stunt almost got him laughed out of the medical community and thrown out of the house by his wife. Eventually it earned him a Nobel Prize. I learned from him that sometimes skirting, or even flouting, rules is the best route to success.

From the former CEO of Pets.com, who presided over the most famous flop in the history of the internet, I drew lessons about how to access the courage and drive it takes to bounce back from failure. Julie Wainwright, now wiser and more mature, is quietly building a business that has far eclipsed the success of Pets.com at its peak.

Steve Kerr, coach of the NBA's Golden State Warriors, told me how he taught himself and others not to allow the fear of making mistakes to limit a willingness to take risks in pursuit of growth. He's led the Golden State Warriors from being simply a good team to winning two NBA titles in three years. In his second year, he took them to the best record in NBA history. From an executive who convinced her bosses at CVS to shut down a $2 billion tobacco business, I found evidence that unsafe thinkers can influence conservative cultures and lead them to make dramatic changes. The risky and counterintuitive move to end cigarette sales became a huge financial and social win for the drug chain.

When I began making my list of unsafe thinkers, I subscribed to the popular notion that such rebels are naturally inclined to defy norms, that they are, as a famous Apple ad dubbed them, "the crazy ones," who just think differently than the rest of us. It seemed most likely to me that they followed their guts and pushed past boundaries with ease—that they didn't fear ridicule or failure. I discovered instead a group of people who had learned to continually face their anxiety—to accept a high degree of discomfort with the risks they were taking and the reactions of critics—in order to challenge themselves. Most of them had gone off course many times. They'd also often gotten stuck in the same kind of traps I found myself in and were still wrestling with their own impulses to take the safe route.

As I learned how off base the prevailing cultural narrative about innovators being "the crazy ones" was, I gained hope. I knew I had to embrace unsafe thinking, and now I saw that it was possible to nurture and master the will and ability to do so. This book shares all I've learned, from firsthand stories and from science, about how to do just that.

INTRODUCTION:
THE PATH TO *UNSAFE THINKING*

Unsafe thinking: The ability to meet challenges with a willingness to depart from standard operating procedures; to confront anxiety, tolerate criticism, take intelligent risks, and refute conventional wisdom—especially one's own views—in order to achieve breakthroughs.

In a rapidly changing world, unsafe thinking is an indispensable skill. But it doesn't come naturally because the basic structures of the human mind prejudice us against changing ourselves and how we approach problems. In fact, the more we gain experience and expertise, the more we tend to stick to familiar approaches. This is in part because we overrely on a decision-making tool that psychologists call the "hill-climbing heuristic." In pursuing solutions to challenges, this subconscious rule of thumb tells us that at each decision point, we should choose the next step that seems to lead most directly toward our goal, which usually means opting for tried-and-true routines. We produce the sequel to last summer's blockbuster. We devote most of our research and development to an incremental upgrade of a proven product. We send out the same fund-raising letter that worked so well last year. We copy our most successful competitors. The problem is that in changing environments, hill climbing, as shown time and again, leads to mediocrity.

And hill climbing is not the only unhelpful mental shortcut we have to contend with. It's just one of dozens of quirks of the human psyche, implanted through evolution, that make us favor safety and familiarity. A need to project authority and surety instead of admitting we need to ask more questions, an involuntary drift toward conformity when working in groups, and a knack for internalizing conventional wisdom until it appears to be our own gut instinct are but a few of the tendencies that prevent us from forging and then sticking to new paths. Ironically, the pull of safe thinking gets strongest when we're in unknown territory that requires new approaches. As our standard operating procedures begin to fail us, the discomfort of uncertainty and fear of failure push us even more urgently to seek safety.

At these times, safe thinking, ironically, can be quite dangerous. It leads to failures of all sorts—for individuals in their lives and careers, for once market-leading companies, and for society as a whole. Medical surveys show that when doctors recommend critical lifestyle changes, up to 70 percent of us choose to stick to our comfortable, unhealthy ways. Gallup reports that more than two-thirds of Americans are disengaged at work. They have settled for the safety of a job that doesn't excite them—and they're sometimes miserable in—rather than risk pursuing a passion. The value of their untapped creative potential is beyond measure.

We're even modeling safe thinking for our children in the American educational system, which is still, despite ample evidence that it's not working, teaching to the test. Thanks to more than a decade of "test and punish" rules that fire teachers and close schools that don't meet standards, American students are falling further behind on basics, while measures of student creativity (the most important competitive skill of the future) are plummeting, threatening to produce yet another generation of safe thinkers. The most common response to these disappointing results? More standards and testing.

While science tells us we face an uphill battle in changing ourselves and our institutions, it also offers plenty of reasons for hope. Over the past several decades, the science of creativity has undergone a revolution. Where once creativity was assumed to be a fixed trait that we can't influence, more recent research tells us we have far more control when it comes to being far more creative.

Harvard psychologist Teresa Amabile began her illustrious career with a rather simple experiment involving a small group of elementary school students, some art supplies, and the help of her two sisters—the only people she could afford to hire at the time.

Amabile organized two parties for the students, who were asked to make collages at both. At one party, the children were told their work would be judged and that the best would win a prize. At the other party, they were told that they'd all enter a raffle at the end that would determine who won rewards for their work. Amabile then took the collages to three professional artists for independent evaluation. The judges unanimously determined that the collages made by the group not expecting to be judged were significantly more creative.

The kids produced better creative work when there was no incentive to do so. These results had enormous implications in Amabile's view and gave her an inkling of a theory that she wanted to develop further. But her mentors advised that, as a woman trying to crack into the notoriously male-dominated field of experimental psychology, she not pursue the work further. It was too far outside the mainstream of research, they told her. It would kill her career prospects. Thankfully Amabile is, herself, an unsafe thinker. She plunged ahead.

In experiment after experiment, she found that the prospects of both reward and punishment quash creative output, while those who engage in work from intrinsic motivation, because they find pleasure in it, are consistently more creative. These findings on motivation and creativity would become widely influential, but they taught Amabile an even more important lesson: individuals' creativity can be enhanced or depressed. We're not just naturally either creative artists or analytical accountants. Certain factors can change our creative ability, and just as Amabile did at her art parties, we can control them.

As Amabile extended her research, she discovered that there are a total of four key components in boosting creativity. Her widely accepted "confluence theory" asserts that when we confront a creative challenge, our ability to break from the status quo to discover novel and useful solutions comes largely down to whether

- we are driven from within to solve a problem.

- we have developed deep knowledge relevant to the problem we're working on. To avoid hitting constant dead ends, we need to know what's been tried before, what's worked, and what's failed.

- we approach the problem through what Amabile describes as a creative workstyle, meaning that we are willing to break old habits, to entertain unfamiliar ideas, and even to break rules.

- the social environment in which we work is conducive to creativity. A management focus on mitigating risk, overly rigid procedures, and politics that pit colleagues against one another can easily squash creativity.

Amabile's findings offer an evidence-based road map for increasing our ability to think beyond the boundaries of safety, but as I tried to apply them to my own conundrum, I quickly discovered that acting on them raises tricky difficulties.

Take intrinsic motivation: the fact of working life is that most of us can't escape outside pressures. We have to please others with our work, be it our bosses or clients or customers, and we have to meet schedules not of our own making. Along the way, we've all got to do at least some work that we just don't find intrinsically motivating, even when the larger mission aligns completely with our passions. Can we optimize our intrinsic motivation, I wondered, even while staying mindful of external pressures?

What about the need for deep knowledge? My own experience as a so-called expert had convinced me that expertise can be a terrible thinking trap. I'd also read a recent study showing that just believing we're experts on a subject makes us more prone to basic factual errors. Given that, I wondered, how can we both build up and draw on expertise and yet not let it blind us to any novel possibilities we should entertain?

Perhaps most challenging: How do we make room for casting aside convention and experimenting with new ideas, given the enormous time and productivity pressures we're under? The management cultures and systems of most organizations squelch our freedom to challenge conventional wisdom and take risks. We can be subject to ridicule, resentment, and even reprisals at work when we rock the boat. How can we cope with anxiety about, and often outright fear of, these possible consequences? And for those of us who are managing teams we'd like to free from these shackles, as I was, how can we do so without tearing the whole company down and starting again?

It took me several years of research, experimentation, and failure to find a path that—I can now confidently say, based on the science and my own experience—can lead us out of the myriad traps of safe thinking to more open, creative, innovative, and joyful ways of operating. Though I've learned along the way to be wary of too much structure, I'll offer a little here as a road map for the journey ahead.

I've organized the book in six parts. Each explores a key component of unsafe thinking and practices that help us overcome the impediments to its use. While many of the tools and actions I've identified take deliberate practice before they begin to feel natural and show results, I can attest that they have provided fuel for my own work. They have allowed me to regain my creative edge and unlocked the creativity of those around me.

Part 1, "Courage," explores the role discomfort, and sometimes outright fear, plays in trapping us in safe thinking. I examine some pernicious myths about anxiety and provide ways to accept, even welcome, the feelings of discomfort that come from challenging the status quo. While many pathways are open to us when we decide to break our old thinking patterns, we can't take the first steps down any of them without the foundation of courage.

Part 2, "Motivation," looks at the energy we need to sustain experimentation with new and uncomfortable approaches to our work, even in the face of setbacks. It goes beyond the usual either/or view of intrinsic and extrinsic motivation and reveals simple means of harnessing the power of both in order to keep creative drive at a consistently high level.

Part 3, "Learning," untangles the seeming paradox that while we need expertise to do successful creative work, we often suffer a decline in learning and performance once we become experts. I show how to reap the advantages of expertise while retaining the nimble thinking and curiosity of a beginner.

Part 4, "Flexibility," provides insights into the power and limits of intuition and the advantages of generating ideas that seem counterintuitive, even ridiculous, to most but in fact contain hidden genius.

Part 5, "Morality," looks at the challenging notion that a strong commitment to do the "right" thing can sometimes be a dangerous commitment to do the same old thing. We'll discover the creativity-enhancing practices of intelligent disobedience and look at why we need more friends who look like enemies.

Finally, Part 6, "Leadership," focuses on working with others and breaking through the social pressures that work against creativity. We'll look at techniques for leading teams, whether you're an officially recognized leader or not, to a more consistent practice of unsafe thinking.

As I've explored the timeless tensions between predictability and innovation, structure and freedom, safety and risk, I've discovered that success lies not in any preordained rules or predetermined ways of breaking them. The breakthroughs of unsafe thinkers often lie in using all the tools available. Rationality and creativity, intuition and analysis, intrinsic and extrinsic drive, expert and beginner mind-sets, these are all essential aspects of human thinking. The most adaptive of us rely on those tools that come most naturally and intentionally work to hone those they are less naturally inclined to use.

This whole-brain way of operating is not automatic or instantly achieved. It seems to me, however, to be urgently needed in an era when automatic and simple solutions, appealing as they may be, are unsuited to the challenges we face. We are confronting social, technological, and ecological problems unimaginable to our ancestors. We also have, for the first time, opportunities to finally eradicate poverty and most diseases while designing far more just communities. Safe thinkers relying on standard approaches won't overcome these challenges or seize these opportunities.

I hope the stories of unsafe thinkers and the science I present will inspire you to experiment with practices that will unlock your own unsafe thinking potential and, if you work within a team, the potential of those with whom you collaborate. My journey into the world of unsafe thinking has shown it to be the route not only to satisfying success in work but to a more fulfilled, exciting, and joyful life.

PART 1

COURAGE

CHAPTER 1

The Safe Thinking Cycle

*Why we stick to our guns
even when we know we shouldn't*

I t's 2015 when I arrive in Austin, Texas, at an intimate gathering of about one hundred CEOs who are there to share their stories of challenge and breakthrough. I've made the trip on a hunch that catching someone in the midst of crisis will reveal insights that stories told after the fact simply won't capture. And one of the planned speakers, I know, is deeply in trouble. As we in the audience take our seats, the anticipation and tension in the room are palpable. Other speakers have shared difficult struggles, but this are the main event.

Whole Foods founder and co-CEO John Mackey sits in front of an extravagant display of plants and flowers meant to communicate well-being and serenity, but his face shows the strain of attempting to match the mood of the backdrop. Nervous whispers ripple through the crowd.

Whole Foods's stock price has plummeted more than 40 percent over the past six months as the growth trajectory of the $15 billion grocery store chain has started to flatten. It seems clear to analysts that the business is running out of market, and Mackey has recently offered compensation packages for employees willing to leave—2,000 have accepted. At the same time, the brand—once so admired—has suddenly come under serious fire. A campaign by the animal rights group PETA, an explosion of social media buzz about high-priced products, and accusations of mismeasurement by the New York State Department of Consumer Affairs have hit almost simultaneously. The press and public have been piling on the derision so quickly that it's been almost impossible to track.

Mackey calls the attacks on the brand "fake news." But the man who founded Whole Foods as a single store thirty-seven years earlier is clearly taking the crisis personally. He begins by describing his original dream to bring healthy food to communities across America and how he surprised himself with his success. Then he discusses how painful it's been to see the company's prospects suddenly turn. "Staying open, knowing something new is trying to birth itself is hard when everyone's screaming at you," Mackey says somberly. Then, referring to himself and co-CEO Walter Robb, he says, "Check in with us in a year. Either a new butterfly will have emerged or we won't be here."

That last comment elicits a quiet gasp from the audience. The stakes are so high that he's openly talking about being removed from his own empire. But it's the first part of Mackey's statement that intrigues me: It's hard to stay open when everyone's screaming at you.

Mackey has expressed one of the key difficulties of changing our thinking when the situation demands it. When facing an unfamiliar challenge, we often know we need to open our minds to a wider field of possible solutions because the status quo clearly will not suffice. At the same time, the threat we feel switches our brains into survival mode, which tends to make us cling to the familiar and engage in safety-seeking behavior. This occurs not only in the face of major threats but also in everyday moments, such as when a project flounders as we're approaching a deadline, when a relationship with a key collaborator turns sour, or when a work product is unexpectedly rejected.

You've probably already been through some version of Mackey's struggle to open yourself to new and creative solutions under pressure, but to see how easily it can arise, take a moment to try a simple experiment on yourself. Grab a pen and paper and try to solve the following puzzle, known as the cheap necklace problem:

Initial Status   Goal Status

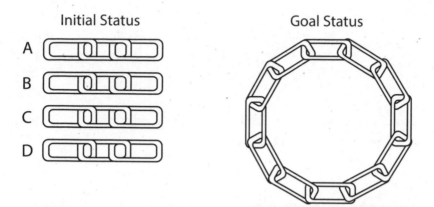

Imagine you want to create a closed necklace out of four chains made up of three links each. Opening a link costs you two cents. Closing a link back up costs three. Your goal is to create this necklace for no more than fifteen cents. Give yourself five minutes to solve it.

Open a link: two cents
Close a link: three cents
Goal: Spend fifteen cents

In test after test, only about 3 percent of people crack the cheap necklace problem. If you tried to solve it, you had a bit of a head start over most test takers because by reading this chapter, you're already primed to think you should try not to narrow your focus on an obvious solution too quickly. Still, given the time pressure, I expect the simple yet counterintuitive solution eluded you. Your mind quickly jumped to what seemed the most direct solution: break some of the end segments and try to link them up. It *must* be right.

Long after this strategy proves futile, people stick with it, only increasing their fixation as the time ticks away.

Ready for the answer? The only way to make the necklace for fifteen cents or less is to start with what feels like a risky step backward. Break all three links on one segment (say segment A), which costs six cents. Six cents gone, no obvious progress.

Step1
Break all the links in Segment A. Cost = 6¢

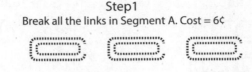

Now, one of those links can form a clasp to connect B to C. Close it up for three cents, and you're at nine.

Step 2
Link Segment A to Segments B and C, then close the open link. Cost = 3¢ (Total 9¢)

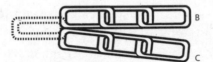

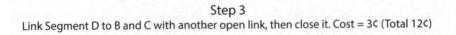

Take your second broken link and attach C and D to each other. Close that link up, and you're at twelve.

Step 3
Link Segment D to B and C with another open link, then close it. Cost = 3¢ (Total 12¢)

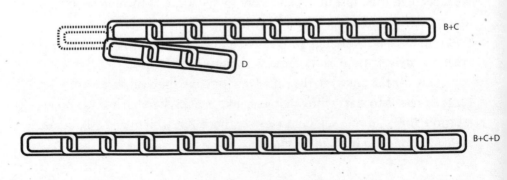

Take the final broken link and attach the two long segments to make a closed necklace for fifteen cents.

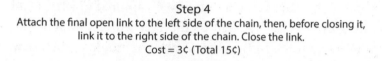

Step 4
Attach the final open link to the left side of the chain, then, before closing it, link it to the right side of the chain. Close the link.
Cost = 3¢ (Total 15¢)

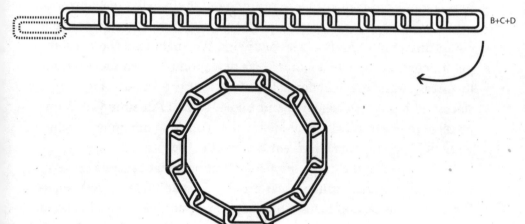

B+C+D

There's nothing inherently complicated about the solution, but in searching for it, most people just loop from what seems the obvious starting point around and around in frustration, trying the same approach. Time expires without their trying anything new. And they usually never consider the counterintuitive step of spending nine cents without making direct progress. Even when given hints that they can only succeed by trying novel and nonobvious approaches, people only nod and smile, instantly returning to their fixations. These experiments teach us that we fixate on safe thinking even when the stakes are extremely low. In this case, the anxiety and stress are minute, perhaps barely noticeable. But even at those low levels, a desire to stick to your guns is extraordinarily difficult to overcome.

Programmed to Seek Safety

So what's happening? Why do we fixate so easily? The pernicious dynamic of clinging to the familiar and safe is captured in what I call the safe thinking cycle. The first step of the cycle, threat awareness, gets triggered in many ways. In the cheap necklace problem, threat awareness comes from realizing we're running out of time. In the real world, we feel it when we get negative sales information, a customer or client complains, or our boss criticizes our work. We might read about a competitor coming out with an impressive new product. Even success leads to threat awareness, paradoxically, because it propels us onto bigger stages, with greater challenges and higher stakes. Put simply, it is impossible to live our lives, let alone try to accomplish anything of value, without triggering threat awareness along the way.

In step two of the cycle, the perception of threat causes a spike in what neuroscientists call cortical arousal, a state of increased wakefulness, vigilance, and focus. Of course, some cortical arousal is often of great value. We need it to react quickly and decisively to physical threats, for example. But a low arousal state is better for creative thinking. In low arousal, the brain apportions its resources to a wide variety of neural and physiological functions, such as digestion, cellular repair, and the filing away of long-term memories. With all our cognitive systems running at normal, we're free to let our attention roam to where our curiosity takes it, and this fosters creative insights.

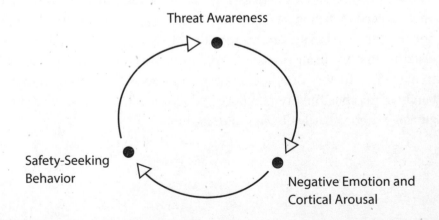

Threat Awareness

Negative Emotion and
Cortical Arousal

Safety-Seeking
Behavior

Thomas Edison, ingeniously, found a way to harness the creative power of extremely low arousal states. He would sit down for a nap in a chair, arms hanging over the sides and a metal ball in each hand. On the floor, he'd place a metal pan. As he drifted toward lower and lower arousal, his brain would present images and ideas unavailable to his conscious mind. But if he fell asleep, the balls would drop, hitting the pans and awakening him in time to record his ideas. He credited these dreamlike images as the source of many of his greatest inventions.

When we confront a challenge that feels threatening, we no longer have the option of staying consistently in low arousal. We are programmed by evolution to respond with high arousal because of the need for speed of action in dealing with many of the threats our early ancestors faced. This response goes way back to the days when confrontations with large predators on the African savannah were common. Imagine you're walking along in a low arousal state, looking around for something for dinner. With urgency low, you are free to scan and take your time searching broadly. But if a predator leaps into your path, your arousal level soars. Stress hormones, such as cortisol and adrenaline, get released, and your attention narrows. Your body also shuts down any unnecessary processes so that blood can flow directly to your muscles and your visual cortex, enabling you to meet the threat. Your vision focuses on the beast, and you are completely engaged with the need to act immediately. Neuroscientists have shown that high cortical arousal actually turns off two regions of the brain that are critical to our ability to think about the future. Who needs to expend energy on tomorrow when you might die right now? Our brains tell us there's time only to fight or flee. This is why cortical arousal is highly adaptive when it comes to surviving in the face of life-threatening danger. But in confronting creative challenges, this response turns against us, hampering our consideration of a wider range of options.

Take the case of a new competitive threat at work, say, from a fast-emerging new technology. Though we may perceive, and perhaps even outwardly declare, that our old ways of operating aren't adequate for this new challenge, and we may feel a desire, like Mackey, to "open up," our brains scream at us to shut down our range of options and take safety-seeking action. These are short-term fixes that we believe will hold off the threat and lower our anxiety. We find ourselves saying things like, "Let's do what worked last time for those guys" or "Let's fix this quickly before it gets out of hand." We tell ourselves that once we've handled the immediate threat, we'll have the luxury of being more expansive.

Unfortunately, we're unwittingly priming the cycle to repeat. Following an old course of action in the face of new challenges sets us up for even more threat and thus more anxiety and arousal.

A series of studies by psychologists Robert Yerkes and John Dodson, who mapped the relationship between arousal and performance, demonstrated the negative effects of this cycle. The now widely accepted Yerkes-Dodson law states that for a while, arousal and performance increase hand in hand. Arousal motivates us to do difficult things. But if the problem one is solving is complex or unfamiliar, requiring more creativity than brute force, they part ways. Past a certain point, arousal increases, and performance plummets. When John Mackey talks about the difficulty of staying open while everyone is screaming at him, he's talking about hitting that divergence.

High arousal won't help Mackey with the threat he's confronting as he speaks to the audience about Whole Foods's travails. The challenge to save his company is not a fight-or-flight physical threat. He might face shame, regret, and loss of personal wealth if he fails to guide Whole Foods past its obstacles. But he won't go hungry, and he certainly won't die. The problem is that our bodies respond to all senses of threat through the same mechanisms with which we responded to lion attacks.

Threats to our jobs, our position in the world, or our esteem among peers don't look similar to a physical threat in our brains. They look the same. The reason for this also lies in our distant past. Being ostracized from a tribe could lead to death for our early ancestors just as surely as an encounter with a lion. This is likely why, in a study by psychologist Michael Williams of people who had faced social exclusion, nearly all of them said they would rather have experienced physical abuse than ostracism.

It also explains why, as John Mackey divulges to the crowd before him in Austin, he must fight a strong impulse to narrow his focus and act quickly rather than opening up and widening his field of options. His biology is pushing him to swim for safe shores. One expedient option might be to concentrate on beating down his detractors through a PR war, attempting to eliminate the threat without addressing the inherent problems in the company's business model and operations. Indeed, throughout the talk, he does occasionally drift into railing against his detractors as if talking himself into pursuing such a path. Or he might fall back on strategies he used to build the company decades ago. Leaders in Mackey's situation often become obsessed with the lessons they learned from past successes and failures. Instead Mackey is working hard to stay open to new ideas.

As the hour-long conversation at the gathering comes to a close, Mackey explicitly expresses resolve to resist his instinctive impulses: "You want to run to safety, but there is no safety in business these days," he concludes.

As I walk out into the warm Texas evening, I have a hunch that this crisis won't be the defining chapter in Mackey's story. Indeed, when I catch up with him later that night, he shares his plans to launch a completely new kind of Whole Foods, a chain of downscale markets catering to customers who can't afford to shop at his high-priced stores. As premium pricing lies at the heart of his thirty-seven-year-old business model, this new approach sounds anything but incremental and familiar.

Mackey's story, of course, didn't unfold exactly according to any expected script. Shortly after we spoke, he would launch his downscale stores, but pressure for growth, especially from activist investors, would continue. In 2017, Amazon purchased Whole Foods for $13.7 billion in cash, with the agreement that Mackey would stay on as Whole Foods's leader. After the deal, he was upbeat about his prospects. "We are going to completely change grocery retailing," he told me. Despite the ongoing pressure that pushed him toward a sale, I heard in Mackey's words the ongoing determination to stay open to new possibilities, not to get locked into operating in ways he'd always known.

CHAPTER 2

Fear as Fuel

*How to embrace anxiety
and break the safe thinking cycle*

"Here's to the crazy ones," the voice of actor Richard Dreyfus proclaims reverently, while the faces of geniuses like Pablo Picasso, Amelia Earhart, and Mahatma Gandhi flash on-screen. They're "the misfits. The rebels. The troublemakers. . . . They're not fond of rules and they have no respect for the status quo." Only the "people who are crazy enough to think they can change the world," Dreyfus reminds us, "are the ones who do."

Apple's 1997 Think Different ad sums up the joys and rewards of smashing boundaries in thirty poetic seconds. The notion that creative breakthrough is the special province of a small elite with an inborn inclination to break rules and ignore social pressures to conform seems intuitively right. While most of us must contend with anxiety and fixation, these rebels know no such struggle.

The reality of the experience of defying convention, however, is often quite different.

On a closer look at the life of one of the "crazy ones," Mahatma Gandhi, we immediately see how unnatural the struggle to go against the grain can be, even for someone who seems to have been at serene peace with it. Gandhi, now a global symbol of courage in the face of danger, wrestled mightily with the fear of not fitting in and being judged. In his autobiography he wrote, "I used to be very shy and avoided all company. My books and my lessons were my sole companions." He would even run home from school "because I could not bear to talk to anybody," afraid "lest anyone should poke fun at me."

Well into adulthood, Gandhi suffered debilitating shyness. In his twenties, while studying law in England, he joined the London Vegetarian Society and became a respected leader of the group. But even on that small public stage, he often had to abandon a speech he was giving, passing his notes to a colleague to finish. The man who went on to lead marches of hundreds of thousands and deliver stirring speeches before massive throngs wrote that his anxiety never fully left him. "When I paid a social call, the presence of half a dozen or more people would strike me dumb," he wrote. "I hesitated whenever I had to face strange audiences and avoided making a speech whenever I could."

Gandhi never became entirely comfortable with social interaction, but he came to see his struggles with himself as an important source of his power. He wrote that his work in confronting his anxiety and pushing himself into the uncomfortable zone of public appearance was the basic training that prepared him to put his life on the line to confront injustice. Though he never lost his fear, he did reframe it, coming to see it as a strength. As he grew older, Gandhi spoke of his shyness, which had once brought him tremendous shame, as one of his key assets. To his trait of speaking hesitatingly and slowly, for example, he attributed the fact that he hardly ever regretted a word he had said. That, he reflected, was a key to his leadership.

We all feel anxiety when setting out on a new and uncharted course. How we contend with that anxiety, I have discovered, makes all the difference.

I began my search for ways to get out of the safe thinking cycle with an intuitive assumption that seemed quite reasonable: there's no avoiding threat awareness, but if we can learn not to respond with anxiety, we can interrupt the cycle. I soon realized, however, that like the participants in the cheap necklace experiment, I was attempting to break the wrong link in the chain. Trying to stop ourselves from feeling anxiety only makes the cycle more pernicious.

Psychologists call the act of suppressing negative emotions "experiential avoidance." People spend enormous amounts of energy trying to master the art. But the effort is worse than useless. Experiential avoidance actually has the effect of exacerbating unwanted emotions.

Steven Hayes, a psychologist at the University of Nevada, Reno, who has studied experiential avoidance, says it has a highly bedeviling nature. For situations outside the body, he writes, human beings use a reasonable strategy to shape the world, essentially taking the approach of "If you don't like it, figure out how to get rid of it and get rid of it." But inside the body, the reverse proves to be true. The rule is, he says, "If you aren't willing to have it, you will." In practical terms, this means that if you aren't willing to feel anxiety, you will feel far more anxiety, plus you will begin to live a narrower and more constricted life.

To see this truth in action, let's return to the story of Mahatma Gandhi and his discomfort with drawing attention to himself. Imagine he had chosen not to put himself in situations that triggered his shyness. Would he have led a more constricted life? Immeasurably so. Would he have suffered less from the anxiety of shyness? No. Ironically, as a shut-in full of unrealized potential, Hayes's theory argues, he would have suffered far more.

Researchers have recently provided powerful verification of Hayes's assertion. Scientists recruited seventy college students for an experiment in which they were told that they would be feeling some pain. Half of the participants were told to suppress thoughts of the upcoming procedure for nine minutes. The other half were instructed simply to note their feelings in anticipation of the experiment. Next came the dreaded pain. Each participant was asked to put his or her arm into ice water for a minute. Those in the thought-suppression group reported significantly more pain than those who had been told to simply notice their anxious thoughts ahead of time. Those trying not to feel anxious not only failed to avoid anxiety but had a worse experience of the feared event when it did arrive. It's no wonder that psychologists have been able to show that the simple belief that "anxiety is bad" leads to anxiety disorders and depression.

Rather than trying to avoid or fight our anxiety, those who study its nature say we should learn to become more comfortable with the discomfort of it, which lessens the impulse to react in a fight-or-flight fashion and frees us to be more creative in our responses to challenges.

Teaching ourselves to be comfortable with a bit of discomfort gives us a far better chance of changing habitual patterns and opening space for new possibilities.

But how can we build up this tolerance? By adjusting how we think about anxiety. This is a core finding in psychology known as cognitive theory. Psychologist Aaron Beck, who pioneered the development of the theory, showed that people can learn to manage anxiety and break free from the intensifying cycle of its grip through what he called cognitive restructuring. Cognitive restructuring is a practice of coaching ourselves to think positively rather than negatively about the anxiety we're feeling and the situation we're confronting. Gandhi's life is a testament to the power of learning this skill.

Experiencing profound loneliness and lack of direction in London, where his shyness threatened to overwhelm his prospects of any success, Gandhi returned home to India with the halfhearted ambition of becoming an attorney. Not surprisingly, his fear followed him across the sea and into the courtroom.

His first case in small-claims court, with a mere ten dollars on the line, was straightforward, and Gandhi felt convinced his client would win. But as he stood up to cross-examine the opposing witness, Gandhi recalls, "My heart sank into my boots. My head was reeling and I felt as though the whole court was doing likewise. I could think of no question to ask." Gandhi looked around desperately for support, but as in a scene from a bad dream, he met with laughter from spectators and judge alike. "I sat down and told the agent that I could not conduct the case."

Reeling from failure, financially responsible for a wife and two young children, and hamstrung by his demons, the young attorney fled again, this time to a job in South Africa that seemed to suit perfectly. It was an ocean away from the lawyers and judges in front of whom he had disgraced himself, and the work, he was told, required no special skill. He could hardly fail if he tried.

He was in for a shock. Gandhi arrived at the South African law offices of Dada Abdulla to confront a complex financial case that only someone with a deep understanding of accounting could manage—Gandhi had none. Again he froze. But Gandhi's biographer and friend Eknath Easwaran reports that before he could run once again, the young lawyer had a flash of realization. "Every time that he had run away from failure before, no matter where he went, the same situation always seemed to recur in even more threatening proportions," Easwaran wrote. It was as if the safe thinking cycle suddenly became clear in Gandhi's mind, and with that awareness came a desire to break it.

This time Gandhi threw himself into learning the practice of book-keeping. He dug into every complex detail of the case and soon became its acknowledged expert. In the end, both sides would look to him as something of a sage who had brought the case to a mutually desirable close. Finally, he felt his power and discovered what he would call "the secret of success."

"He began to look on every difficulty as an opportunity for service," Easwaran explains, "a challenge which could draw out of him greater resources of intelligence and imagination."

Through this case, Gandhi began to perceive challenges as chances for growth. One further pivotal event completed his evolution into an unsafe thinker, and doer, extraordinaire.

Sent by his employer across the country by train on a first-class ticket, Gandhi was shocked in the mountain town of Pietermaritzburg when a white passenger complained about the small brown man sitting in the wrong car. Gandhi's ticket said first-class, but by law, he was not allowed to hold that ticket. When the conductor attempted to remove him, Gandhi protested and found himself pushed off the train by force, abandoned to sleep in the deserted train station. It was frigid that evening, and he had neither his overcoat nor his luggage; they had departed on the train that left him behind.

During this long, frozen night, Gandhi confronted his fears. He determined that he could either once again flee a country that disdained him, or he could fight back.

He reminded himself that he had run from uncomfortable feelings too many times into the arms of failure, whereas the one time he had moved toward these feelings with a sense of curiosity and possibility, he had found success. He would call this moment of realization at the train station "the most creative incident" of his life, because in seeing his painful emotions not as threatening but as a sign that he had an opportunity to grow stronger, Gandhi created the space in his psyche to calm down and open up. That led him to devise the practice of satyagraha, the principle of nonviolent resistance, one of the most powerful tools of social protest the world has ever known, which resulted in the triumph of his efforts for Indian independence.

Within months, Gandhi was leading marches of South African Indians in protest of new repressive racial laws. He soon came face-to-face with General Jan Smuts, then colonial secretary.

"I've come to tell you that I am going to fight against your government," Gandhi said quietly but firmly.

"You mean you have come here to tell me that?" the general asked incredulously. "Is there anything more you want to say?"

"Yes," Gandhi replied. "I am going to win. With your help."

These words from a man, in confrontation with overwhelming power, who a couple years earlier couldn't cross-examine a witness in small-claims court. His words convey almost impossible boldness but also truth: he did win, and by the end he had Smuts's help.

Getting Comfortable with Discomfort

How do we begin to create the space, as Gandhi did, for thinking more positively about creative challenges? Cognitive psychology has shown that the simple process of becoming aware that we're having an automatic, emotional reaction and coaching ourselves to accept the feelings rather than trying to avoid them can be extraordinarily powerful. Gandhi may seem an impossible role model, but he's far from alone in learning to see his anxiety as a guide to growth. Many of the unsafe thinkers I've met have pulled off the feat of consciously interrupting their own thought patterns and moving toward discomfort.

Micah White is one of them. He's been in confrontation with politicians, the police, and even mainstream activist organizations who share his politics. He's started campus uprisings and entered war zones. Remember Occupy Wall Street? White helped start the whole thing while working at Adbusters. He's the guy who coined the protest's name and called the first activists to the encampments.

White follows a simple philosophy: never use the same tactic twice. He believes novelty and unexpectedness bring people to the streets and keep the press interested and the police confused. Yet, he too deals with the traps of the safe thinking cycle.

"I've always been an anxious person," he admitted to me. He described wrestling with doubt and uncertainty every time he puts an idea out in the world. "But to be successful, I've had to reinterpret what those feelings mean."

Having vowed not to repeat the same resistance tactic twice, White can never allow himself to feel comfortable with what's worked for him in the past. He needs to constantly consider creative and risky ideas. Over the years, reframing his anxiety has given him a critical insight that keeps this source flowing. "I've realized that there's a discomfort you feel just before you come up with a really good idea," he said. "I interpret this discomfort as a positive sign."

With this interpretation, White is interrupting the safe thinking cycle. We cannot avoid anxiety, and we also know that once anxiety triggers cortical arousal, we are biologically at an enormous disadvantage in trying to find creative solutions. But if we can welcome a bit of discomfort with a belief that it is a necessary signal of the potential for growth, we can feel the cortical arousal, give it a moment (or a day) to pass, and then retake control of our actions.

White has reframed anxiety as desirable because it indicates that he has pushed beyond the boundaries of tried, true, and dead ideas. Instead of bravely suffering through his discomfort, he has learned to use it to fuel his creativity. Such reframing served him particularly well when the Occupy movement collapsed before meeting any of its goals. Instead of blaming others or distancing himself from the movement, he immediately began to research the causes and lessons of what he calls a "productive failure" in order to plan his next campaigns of resistance.

The findings and techniques I offer in the following chapters are challenging. They cause discomfort, and part of us inevitably prefers to learn about these practices from a safe distance, filing them away as interesting ideas rather than pathways to action. But with a foundation of courage and a mind-set that embraces rather than shrinks from anxiety, we can learn to master discomfort and change long-held thinking patters. We'll begin our exploration with the ego-defying practice of challenging your own inner expert and regaining the advantages of the beginner's mind.

COURAGE: KEY TAKEAWAYS

Seek moments of low arousal

Even in times of crisis, we need to give ourselves breaks to allow our minds to explore new possibilities and move beyond stereotypical thinking. Thomas Edison even developed a practice of holding balls above a metal pan to awake him if he drifted into sleep so he could capture insights on the edge of sleep.

How do you step away, even for a few moments, from the fray? Five minutes of meditation? A long shower? A short walk? All have been shown to decrease arousal and open creative possibilities.

Accept anxiety as part of the journey

Remember the students who tried to talk themselves into feeling less pain? They felt more. Steeling yourself against discomfort or avoiding situations that induce it will likely create even more anxiety. Like Gandhi, we gain problem-solving power by looking at difficulties as opportunities to draw more deeply on our intelligence and imagination.

Seek situations that push you beyond your comfort zone. Note your feelings as you experience them. By carefully observing your responses, you'll likely find these experiences to be more valuable and even perhaps enjoyable than comfortable, familiar ones.

Reimagine fear as fuel for creativity

Occupy cofounder Micah White said, "I've realized that there's a discomfort you feel just before you come up with a really good idea. I interpret this discomfort as a positive sign." How you interpret your feelings makes all the difference.

When you feel fear, remind yourself that it might indicate that you're on the edge of a creative breakthrough. That's not wishful thinking. That's science.

PART 2

MOTIVATION

CHAPTER 3

Mastering Motivation

How to energize yourself and others to stay on the edge

O n November 8, 2000, Julie Wainwright's husband woke her at 4 a.m. to tell her that he couldn't live with her stress any longer. He wanted a divorce. For Wainwright, this was only the beginning of what was already slated to be a heart-breaking day. She walked out to her car and drove to her office, where she began the process of laying off more than one hundred employees and shutting down a company that she had nurtured from a seedling and that had been worth $330 million a year earlier. Wainwright's own stake had fallen from $10 million to nothing. Gone. Like her reputation and now her marriage.

The fact that other dot-coms were closing left and right that year might have softened the blow, but in Wainwright's case, it only made things worse. Her business was already the poster child for dot-com excess, and it was now certain to be the media's favorite punching bag in the wider industry collapse. Yes, the company had lost $147 million over the last twenty months, but that was hardly unusual in the era of dot-com busts. Wainwright's fall was so easy to gloat over because of the damn puppet. In 1999, Pets.com had spent a couple million dollars on a Super Bowl ad featuring a low-fi and annoying canine reporter made from a sock. The puppy had become symbolic of Silicon Valley's unorthodox, youth-focused, irreverent approach to business, now re-vealing itself as a sham. In the next few days, Wainwright would have to call the police to get the swarming press off her property.

On this traumatic day, she was forty-two years old, the same age her mother had been when multiple sclerosis began to damage her brain and initiated a twenty-year slide into suffering and ultimately death. Wainwright says she had pushed so hard to succeed in business in reaction to the limitations she had watched life place on her mother. "I was determined to be the biggest person I could be and live as fully as possible," she says. But as Pets.com became "the biggest joke in the valley" and "tech's biggest flop," Wainwright had begun what felt like her own slide toward the valley of death.

"I felt lethargic, could not experience joy and was emotionally drained all of the time," she told San Jose's *Mercury News*.

I met Wainwright seventeen years later under very different circumstances. She is now running a far less famous but far more successful business than Pets.com ever was. The Real Real is an online consignment shop for luxury goods. Customers send in their unwanted dresses, purses, shoes, and jewelry to be verified, appraised, and sold. Not everyone, Wainwright admits, understands the niche she's created.

"The other day someone asked me, 'How's your online dress store going?' I responded, 'You mean my half-a-billion-dollar online dress store?'" Wainwright laughed. Indeed, the company has moved that much merchandise over the past year, and The Real Real is now valued at over $2 billion.

I found my way to Wainwright as I began to investigate motivation and the sources of energy required to continually think and act outside standard operating procedure. I was searching for examples, beyond the laboratory, that would reveal where people find the drive to persevere through the many-staged act of creation and to pick themselves up from the inevitable failures that are part of the process. It's well known, of course, that successful entrepreneurs generally have an ability to accept and bounce back from failure. But because Pets.com suffered such a spectacular implosion, I was eager to ask Wainwright how she had managed to rejoin the fray, facing a community of investors so intimately familiar with her humiliation and throwing herself into risky invention one more time. Was it pride and a need to reestablish her reputation? A desire to regain her lost fortune? An insatiable love of the game of business?

I found that Wainwright draws energy from all these motivational sources—and more: from building a legacy, creating an enormously valuable company, reducing landfill waste by keeping valuable goods in circulation, proving that women can succeed as entrepreneurs, and experiencing the delightful process of creation. As soon as one of these motivations popped into her mind during our conversation, she headed off on a passionate tangent about its absolute importance to her. Wainwright calls herself "insatiable" for all of it.

For a year after Pets.com collapsed, Wainwright stayed out of sight. Then she slowly attempted to rebuild her career. Within a few years, she had started an online knowledge-sharing tool that quickly went under, another setback that might have been devastating but paled in comparison to her public Pets.com meltdown. Then one day Wainwright walked into a high-end boutique with a wealthy friend in Marin. Her companion made a beeline for the back where the consignment goods were displayed. At first Wainwright was confused. Why would someone want used stuff? But when she saw the objects of her friend's obsession, she realized these high-end items that had withstood the test of time were the most beautiful goods in the store. This got her wheels turning quickly. What were they doing at the very back, out of sight, she wondered? Why were they being guarded like a shameful secret?

"I knew then I had something huge," she told me. Sure, Wainwright realized, you can buy and sell used stuff on eBay, but who would spend $5,000 on something that might be counterfeit? eBay just isn't set up to verify goods and doesn't want to be in that business. In the gap left open by online marketplaces, Wainwright saw an irresistible opportunity.

She says her enjoyment for the game of finding and exploiting a business niche overwhelmed her trepidation about putting herself back into the arena. She says of starting a business, "It's highly creative, and it's really analytical. I think it's one of the sexiest things you can do. It's so much fun." She also derives endless pleasure, she says, from the constant learning that building a business requires. These are the kinds of motivation that Teresa Amabile highlights as keys to creativity, motivations in which the act of working on a problem is itself the reward. They are indispensable to creativity.

But this love of creating and business building gets equal real estate in Wainwright's mind with other sources of motivation that have less to do with the work than the rewards she might gain through success. "There are very few women, if any, that have taken a multi-billion-dollar company public," she points out. "It's a whole different thing to start from nothing and be at the helm of taking it all the way." Clearly she wants to experience that thing. Wainwright insists she's not driven to silence her critics from the Pets.com days, but it's apparent that she thinks about leaving her mark and getting the credit she deserves. "I want this company to live on and endure," she says. When I ask her why, she says, "Because it deserves a place." Reading between the lines, I think she means because *she* deserves a place. And seeing what she's built from the ashes of gut-wrenching failure, I find it hard to imagine that she'll be stopped before she gets it.

◇◇◇◇◇◇◇◇

When I met Wainwright, I'd been familiar with the popular understanding of motivation. No doubt you've heard it in some form too. It tells us that to sustain our energy while taking the risk of breaking with the herd and to pick ourselves up from failure, we must be driven primarily by passion for the work we're doing, or as psychologists say, we must be intrinsically motivated. Intrinsic motivation brings to mind the master craftsman, the dedicated teacher, or the visionary artist. On the other hand, the popular understanding goes, the energy of those focused on money, reputation, or impact (motivators known as extrinsic) will most likely flag once the going gets tough. Thus, it would seem that we must find a constant source of commitment necessary for unsafe thinking in intrinsic motivation. But is it really that simple?

This notion doesn't come out of nowhere. Teresa Amabile shook the world of creativity research by demonstrating how children lose their creative edge when offered a reward for their work. And other evidence abounds. The London School of Economics studied fifty-one companies using pay-for-performance plans and found that these bonuses actually decreased employee effectiveness. Studies of fine artists have rated the paintings clients paid them to do as significantly less creative than their noncommissioned works. The widely understood takeaway: intrinsic, good; extrinsic, bad.

Compelling as the studies are, I found this message disempowering and difficult to match to real-world experience. Can we really expect to achieve a state of pure intrinsic motivation without quitting our jobs and heading for the Himalayas? And don't those, like Wainwright, who both love what they do and also crave recognition or money do plenty of great things? After all, the majority of brilliant work doesn't get produced by hermetic artists, locked in their studios, who care nothing for the opinions of the public. Geniuses like Isaac Newton and Charles Darwin were deeply driven by the love of their studies but also highly concerned about the praise and criticism of their peers and the public. Similarly, every social entrepreneur I know is at least as passionate about having an impact on the world as about his or her day-to-day work.

Don't most of us actually toggle back and forth, I wondered, between both intrinsic and extrinsic forms of motivation? And if so, might there be ways to optimize our mix of motivators to give ourselves the fuel we need to stay unsafe?

Recent science offers powerful answers. Yes, there are times when a focus on rewards can be absolutely deadly. But there are smart ways to use intrinsic and extrinsic motivation together to amplify the energy and commitment required to keep ourselves in the demanding zone of challenge and creativity.

Discovering Intrinsic Motivation

Today's orthodoxy is often yesterday's heresy, and that's certainly the case with the science of motivation. Before intrinsic motivation became widely accepted as the gold standard, it was believed not to exist at all.

The year is 1949, and Harry Harlow is running a primate behavior laboratory at the University of Wisconsin, investigating how monkeys learn. He subscribes, like everyone else at the time, to the prevailing behaviorist theory of motivation.

Animals, the thinking goes, have reward centers in their brains that make them feel good when they get things that help them survive and thrive, like food, sex, or protection from their peers. The actions they engage in are designed to win them as much of this stuff as possible and to reap the chemical rewards, such as dopamine, that their brains secrete when they succeed. Humans, as big-brained animals, are no different. Everything we do, we do for food, sex, and safety. So why do we work? Simple: to get money and prestige, which leads to meals, mates, and security. That's true whether you're an accountant or an artist. We're all just seeking what come down to survival-based rewards. Rats run through mazes, monkeys press buttons, and humans pull slot machines and create sonatas, new products, and whole companies all for a little dopamine. There's only one type of motivation, in other words, and it's extrinsic.

Harlow has never thought to question all this. So, when he places a three-step puzzle in the cages of eight rhesus monkeys, he expects they'll try it in the hopes of gaining a reward though he, at first, offers none. The puzzle is novel to the monkeys and requires some deep simian thinking. According to behaviorism, if a monkey spends a bunch of mental energy cracking a problem and gets nothing in return, he will not be motivated to try again.

But the monkeys have other ideas. They fiddle with the puzzles, eventually solving them. Then, like obsessive teenagers with a Rubik's Cube, they solve them again, and again, continually improving their speed and skill. It looks as if the monkeys are actually enjoying the process of mastering the puzzles.

Surprised, Harlow begins to wonder if another kind of motivation might be at play here, which he, for the first time, calls intrinsic motivation. Perhaps the monkeys are driven, he hypothesizes, by the fun and challenge of a difficult problem.

As the monkeys get better and better at puzzle solving, Harlow thinks he can increase their learning even more by adding in a classic extrinsic reward, in this case a raisin. Will the two types of motivation work together? He's floored to discover that the answer is no. Offer a raisin as a reward, and the monkeys are less able to solve the puzzle. They make more errors. They lose interest. It appears that if you offer monkeys a prize for engaging in an inherently enjoyable activity, they become less engaged.

Harlow's experiment was the first stirring of what would become a seismic shock to the world's understanding of motivation. Over the decades, as researchers conducted studies with human subjects to test Harlow's results, one experiment after the next pointed to the counterintuitive finding that when performing anything but the most mechanical tasks, people seem to become less engaged, less effective, and less hardworking when offered a reward.

Decades after these results were published and psychologists did a 180 to embrace the notion that intrinsic motivation not only exists but is often more powerful than extrinsic motivation, we still struggle to take their lesson to heart. Hoping to increase performance, managers continue to push their teams to pursue extrinsic markers of success, often killing their drive and creativity in the process. In the worst cases, such focus can lead to the blossoming of a perverse kind of creativity that undermines the very institutions it is meant to drive forward.

When Motivation Goes Awry

After 2001, the federal No Child Left Behind Act revamped how we incentivize educators across the country. With the aim of raising the bar for all students, schools became subject to a constant regime of standardized tests. Success on these tests became the determinant of teacher careers and even the survival of entire schools.

The school district in Atlanta, Georgia, embraced this focus on metrics with particular vigor, and the test scores of the city's schools began to rise. But while the district was being touted as a success story, teachers and principals found themselves under increasing pressure to perform. If a school increased its scores one year, the expectations would be even higher the next. Principals who missed their numbers were routinely threatened with firing, and they passed the pressure down. One principal forced a teacher who couldn't keep her kids' scores up to crawl under a table during a faculty meeting as a lesson to her peers.

Just as a couple raisins killed the drive of Harlow's monkeys to complete puzzles, a flood of extrinsic motivation redirected Atlanta's educators away from solving the problem of getting children to learn. In 2009, a scandal exploded in the system. Forty-four of Atlanta's fifty-six schools were found to have been cheating on standardized tests. The students weren't cheating; teachers and administrators were. Groups of teachers were breaking into the offices of state testing coordinators, stealing the tests, and bringing them to "erasure parties," where adults carefully corrected student mistakes. Teachers made seating charts to put low-performing students next to their high-performing peers, then subtly let it be known that peeking was OK. Their ingenuity was so refined that hundreds of coconspirators went undetected for more than five years before it all came crashing down. Some of the teachers wound up in prison.

There is something so attractive about setting and reinforcing extrinsic goals that we constantly forget their pitfalls. Even after the Atlanta scandal, school reformers continued to focus on testing. Tim Callahan, a spokesman for the Professional Association of Georgia Educators, warned that the natural intrinsic motivation of teachers was still being systematically undermined. "Our teachers' best qualities—their sense of humor, their love for the subject, their excitement, their interest in students as individuals—are not being honored or valued," he told the *New Yorker*. "Because those qualities aren't measurable."

The vast majority of teachers enter their professions brimming with intrinsic motivation. In the case of Atlanta's public schools, a culture that rewarded, cajoled, and threatened teachers with numbers and measurements not only subverted their natural intrinsic drives but created desperate antisocial behavior that nearly brought the whole system down. It's a cautionary tale about what can happen to any of us if we take something we love and add too much focus on extrinsic motivation to the work.

Creating Motivational Alchemy

Damning as the case is against extrinsic motivation, something fundamental is missing in the popular understanding of it. That something is *why?* Sure, the Atlanta case was an extreme version of replacing intrinsic love of teaching with an extrinsic focus on numbers. But if getting raisins is motivating and solving puzzles is motivating, why can't these types of motivators play nicely together? Why do external rewards so often cancel out the intrinsic love of doing something? For a long time, science didn't have a firm answer. Then a landmark study offered an explanation, opening the door for a much richer understanding of motivation and clues as to how people like Julie Wainwright effectively draw energy from all kinds of motivational sources. It comes down to being aware of and taking conscious control of our motivations.

The study was conducted by three investigators who began to wonder if it might be possible to inoculate people against the negative effects of extrinsic motivation. Up to this point, motivational experiments had treated human subjects much like lab rats, as unwitting victims of experimenters' manipulations. What would happen if you taught people a little about motivation to give them more control over how they respond to incentives? Sixty-eight elementary school students would surprise these researchers as much as the monkeys had surprised Harlow.

The experimenters divided the students into two groups. One would get a motivational vaccine in the form of a short video followed by a discussion with a facilitator. In the video, an eleven-year-old boy speaks with an adult, who asks him about his favorite subject in school. "Well, I like social studies," Tommy replies. "I like learning about how other people live in different parts of the world. It's also fun because you get to do a lot of projects and reports . . . and when I come up with good ideas I feel good." Tommy is explaining, in terms anyone can understand, what it's like to feel intrinsically motivated. Next, the adult asks him about grades and the rewards his parents give him for doing well. "Well, I like to get good grades and when I bring home a good report card my parents always give me money. But that's not what's really important. I like to learn a lot. . . . I work hard because I enjoy it." After watching these videos and discussing their own feelings, the kids joined the noninoculated group, and everyone was invited to tell a creative story. Half the kids, however, were offered a reward for telling the story. The rest were not.

So did the inoculation work? As expected, the kids who didn't see the video but were offered a reward told rather uncreative stories. Extrinsic motivation killed their drive. But when it came to the kids who had learned about motivation, the reward not only didn't hurt them but boosted their performance. The kids who were trained and rewarded were by far the most creative bunch. The simplistic classroom videos might not be as appropriate for adults, but the effect of bringing awareness to the different types of motivation and discussing them with peers applies to everyone.

The study was notable because it achieved its goal of protecting kids from the dangers of extrinsic motivation and unexpectedly offered an even more important lesson for enhancing creativity. It shed new light on the vexing question of why the two types of motivators often don't work well together.

The researchers concluded that when offered rewards in ways that make us feel manipulated, coerced, or controlled—which is how our bosses and society tend to impose extrinsic motivators—we, like the Atlanta teachers, lose motivation. We feel like pawns in someone else's game and give up or act in counterproductive ways. But when we understand the two types of motivation and rewards are offered in an upfront way that doesn't feel manipulative, we can make choices about how we respond to rewards. We come to treat them as fun, enjoyable bonuses rather than tools of control. Thus the external rewards only serve to increase our intrinsic drive.

The conventional idea that rewards are a creativity killer leaves managers, parents, and coaches with few tools to keep those they lead at a high level of creative performance and dooms each of us to the simple hope that our love of our work remains high enough to carry us through. But if we're smart and have established a base of love for what we do, we can use the desire for money, esteem, status, or freedom in just the right way to boost motivation. Amabile uses the term "motivational synergy" to describe the mix of intrinsic and extrinsic incentives we can set up for ourselves or others that nurture rather than destroy energy and drive.

For example, extrinsic rewards that affirm the value of creativity, like giving more creative time, stoke intrinsic motivation in a way that a cash prize doesn't. Intuit, the financial software giant, uses what it calls an "Unstructured Time" reward for top innovators. At Intuit, if you perform at a high level, you'll get significant chunks of time to explore and play wherever your passions lead. Tools like friendly competition between team members or prizes that are small enough not to become the main reason for doing a project also provide a little hit of motivation that can be particularly effective. Even a cash bonus can be productive if the person receiving it has been empowered to help design the bonus structure, casting it as a self-reward for a job well done.

The key takeaway is that if we're intrinsically motivated by our work, we can make good use of the appeal of money, esteem, status, or freedom to further boost motivation as long as we have some understanding of and control over when we're being offered raisins with our puzzles. Raisins are tasty, but they lose their appeal when getting them makes us feel like animals in a lab.

The Right Motivation at the Right Time

Satisfying as I found the concept of constantly combining intrinsic and extrinsic motivation, I still wondered about what I call the slog problem. Even the most important work can't offer a constant stream of intrinsic motivation from start to finish. Identifying problems and brainstorming ideas, both early building stages, are often full of intrinsic pleasure. Tweaking, perfecting, analyzing data, and removing road blocks often occupy far more of our time, and some of these simply don't feel joyful. So what do we do about these stages of creation?

John Cleese, the comic genius and cofounder of the British comedy troop Monty Python, offers a compelling mental road map for how to use various types of motivation at various stages of a project to keep us going.

Cleese says that to be successful with creative endeavors, we've got to work in two different modes, the "open" and "closed" modes.

"The open mode is relaxed, expansive, less purposeful, in which we're probably more contemplative, more inclined to humor which always encompasses a wider perspective. And consequently more playful," he explains in a wide-ranging talk on creativity. "We're not under pressure to get a specific thing done more quickly. We can play. And that is what allows our natural creativity to surface."

Cleese celebrates the open mode and revels in it as long as possible. But he says there's an important role for its opposite. In the closed mode, "we have inside us a feeling that there's lots to be done and we have to get on with it if we're going to get through it all. . . . It's a mode in which we're probably a little impatient, if only with ourselves. It has a little tension in it, not much humor. It's a mode in which we're very purposeful, and it's a mode in which we can get very stressed and even a bit manic, but not creative." The closed mode is often where we need to be when we're in the slog phase of a creative process.

Research shows that when we're in the creative phase of seeking out problems to solve or brainstorming solutions, the phases that call for the open mode, it's best not to distract ourselves from intrinsic enjoyment with extrinsic rewards. We should keep the bonuses, the deadlines, and a focus on competition away from our own and our teams' conscious attention as much as we reasonably can.

For the much less enjoyable closed mode phase, though, some extrinsic motivation can be extremely helpful. When implementation drags out and the fun of creation dissipates, a well-placed and playful reward can reignite one's fire, or that of a team.

Cleese's open/closed distinction is so useful because it helps us to keep in mind which phase of a creative process we're in and either to allow ourselves the time to savor the exploration and learning that's so satisfying or to prod ourselves or our team with some extrinsic motivation, some sweet raisins to keep us going. We can constantly be fine-tuning the motivational mix to fit the demands of the moment. When we do that, we're bringing the kind of conscious attention to motivation that science says gives us a sense of control and excitement about our work.

When I first sat down with Julie Wainwright, she told me she only had a half hour (though we talked for much longer), so I decided to get right to the point. "I'd like to talk about motivation," I told her. "I've been looking at research that says when you love working on something, it becomes a lot easier to succeed."

"That's bullshit," she replied before I could continue. "It's true that you need to love what you do. But it's still hard. It's hard every day. It never gets easy."

Her statement made a strong impression on me and led to a number of questions that a concept like motivational synergy doesn't address. Is it realistic to think we can sustain love, and the intrinsic motivation we derive from it, through a process that is always hard? Don't we ultimately strive for an eventual sense of mastery in our work? Though Wainwright says she has an "aggressive need to overcome obstacles," won't constant challenge eventually wear out the less obsessive among us? In fact, I would learn, a sense of constant difficulty and challenge is not a motivation killer; it's a key ingredient in keeping motivation high and unsafe thinking possible. We turn next to how we can keep ourselves in the zone of challenge without drifting over the edge into a rut of despair.

CHAPTER 4

Finding Your Source

Why we need to love the challenges we face

C am McLeay steers into the mouth of a tributary of the Nile River, gently revving the engine of his small inflatable boat, a wonderfully maneuverable craft known as a Zap Cat. The water is nearly still. The only sound comes from the massive reeds rubbing gently against one another in a light breeze. Then, without warning, a crocodile erupts from the water twenty feet straight ahead. It looks to be at least fifteen feet long. A croc that size can easily flip the boat.

McLeay has just enough time to turn around, but as his hands grip the wheel, he envisions the Zap Cat in mid-maneuver with the lightning-fast predator in pursuit. Not good.

Fighting his first impulse, he instead holds his course and jams the accelerator, charging the animal. The move departs from anything McLeay had contemplated before this moment arose. The boat's engine roars, and the startled croc dives beneath the surface. The blades of the low-hanging outboard motor graze its body, and the boat shudders, but it stays upright.

A few moments later, the croc surfaces thirty feet away. It stares at the boat as if contemplating an attack and then swims off.

That evening, McLeay records the encounter in his diary as yet another harrowing and impossible-to-prepare-for moment in the Ascend the Nile expedition. He and his three partners on the journey hope to travel up the entire length of the river, from where it spills out into the Mediterranean to its farthest source, deep in central Africa, making them the first to chart its full extent. The feat has been attempted from the time of the ancient Egyptians but never achieved.

Every day the Nile tests the team's resolve and ingenuity, throwing unexpected, often life-threatening, challenges their way. On day forty-one they reach the 140-foot Murchison Falls, where the river's waters crash down so fiercely the boats can hardly approach, let alone attempt an ascent. The steep cliffs to either side make a portage impossible.

The team has brought along a machine called a flying inflatable boat (FIB), which looks like a small raft with a glider wing on top and a giant fan hanging off the back. They have a vague idea that if worst comes to worst, they might lash their Zap Cats to the FIB and try to fly up impassable parts of the river. But they hadn't had time to practice the maneuver, and failure could be deadly. After a tricky assembly, Neil McGrigor, the team mechanic, climbs into the contraption and zooms straight at the roaring wall of water. Lifting hesitantly into the air, the makeshift craft wobbles, but then soars, and in moments he's up and over. His landing above the falls will, unexpectedly, prove almost as dangerous as his takeoff. As McGrigor views the pool in which he will touch down, he spots more than a dozen sleeping hippos. They look placid but are in fact some of the most dangerous animals in the world. He brings the craft in as gently as he can, his heart racing.

With each new challenge, the team responds with vigor, cleverly improvising, experimenting with dozens of new approaches to river navigation. Some of their experiments succeed, others fail, but the team's resolve stays firm through the unrelenting obstacles.

Four thousand miles from their launch point in Egypt, the expedition ends deep in a forest of Rwanda, where a mere trickle of water bubbles up from a group of rocks. They declare victory, believing they have found the Nile's true source. They have also taken the world record for the longest river journey.

Beginning in 1857, John Hanning Speke trekked overland for 1,000 miles, arriving diseased and half mad at Lake Victoria, which he marked as the source of the Nile. He never took the next step to find the source of the lake, however, rendering his claim, many believe, incomplete.

Nevertheless, Speke got an obelisk from the Royal Geographic Society. It still stands in London's Kensington Gardens. Credited with solving "the problem of all ages," he became an international hero. But the glory years of exploration are long over. Beyond an admiring article from *National Geographic*, the Ascend the Nile team was barely acknowledged. No parades, no big sponsorship offers, no obelisks.

I spoke extensively with McLeay, trying to understand what made his team so successful in reaching their goal. At first, I was surprised and a little outraged on their behalf by the lack of acclaim they had received. But McLeay told me that his team didn't mind. They weren't looking for money or fame. They made the journey because they love the process of exploring, deadly dangers and all.

"It's these adventures that, for me, make life worth living," McLeay told me.

◇◇◇◇◇◇◇

Every day people get stuck in the face of new and critically important challenges. All too often, they lose their drive to succeed and settle for the mediocre. They fall back on the familiar rather than take the risks needed for success. Why is that? Why is an energetic commitment to a goal and a willingness to do whatever it takes to get there, attitudes on full display in the Ascend the Nile expedition, the exception rather than the rule? And does it have to be?

The obvious answer that McLeay provides, of course, is that his team was brimming with intrinsic motivation. Exploring a river may perhaps appear, by its nature, more intrinsically motivating than solving a vexing business problem. Intrinsic motivation can work wonders on the energy of a team. But rather than just assuming as much, it's worth asking why such an adventure can be so enjoyable for those who engage in it. While we may imagine adrenaline-pumping rapids, the gentle hum of exotic wildlife, and vistas of untouched beauty, the journey was often grueling and consistently life threatening, and the moments of triumph punctuated long stretches of terrible physical discomfort and boredom. If intrinsic motivation means that the reward derives from the journey itself, why exactly was this journey so rewarding when so many other creative journeys feel like a grind?

Psychological science has a surprisingly clear answer to this question. It tells us not simply that a healthy dose of intrinsic motivation is important but where intrinsic motivation actually springs from. And it provides clues for how we might imbue any team's work with focus, energy, and love of the process.

Loving Difficult Things

To understand what the science tells us, let's imagine we're there as part of the Ascend the Nile team, staring up at the imposing Murchison Falls. What's going through our heads? Well, first we recognize that we're facing an extremely high-challenge environment. Nobody's ever gone, or even tried to go, up these falls in a watercraft. We've got our flying inflatable boat, but the idea of attaching it to a Zap Cat and soaring up waterfalls is completely untested. If we choose not to try, our expedition is over. The significant money we've invested is gone and our careers set back. On the other hand, one slipup in our attempt could easily cost lives. (In fact, farther up the river the FIB contraption did crash, nearly killing McGrigor.)

Though the level of challenge we face is extremely high, so is our level of skill. Between us, we have decades of on-the-river experience. McGrigor is an ingenious mechanic. George Heathcote is an African wildlife expert, which will come in handy when navigating those angry hippos. We have emergency medical and survival training.

High challenge and high skill. Psychologist Mihaly Csikszentmihalyi (pronounced "chick-sent-me-high") uses the term "flow" to describe the psychological state we enter when these conditions converge. Through decades of highly influential research, he's shown that this exact combination—more precisely, when the level of challenge just barely exceeds the level of skill—lays the groundwork for producing a state of heightened focus, creativity, and determination. If we add to this mix clear goals and the ability to get consistent feedback on our progress, Csikszentmihalyi has demonstrated, flow consistently emerges. Despite exertion and hard work, people in flow feel a sense of love for the task they are involved in and are far more likely to invent novel and useful solutions. Ask someone who experiences flow in an activity why they do it, and they'll invariably point to the satisfaction they gain from the task itself. Flow is a key source of intrinsic motivation.

The first spark of the idea of flow came to Csikszentmihalyi from his own experience as a rock climber. In a state of high challenge and high skill, with a clear goal at the top of a rock face, he would find himself brimming with the kind of determination and energy he needed to take risks and overcome his natural conservatism. As he sought out others with similar experiences—artists, surgeons, inventors, CEOs—he repeatedly heard descriptions of this type of energetic engagement.

To make flow accessible and achievable, Csikszentmihalyi has created a simple visual representation. It shows a "flow channel," a navigable path that allows one to avoid the fear and helplessness that come from having not enough skill to meet a challenge, on the one hand, and the boredom and apathy that come from having too much skill for the challenge one faces, on the other.

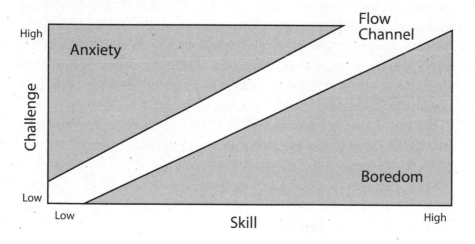

It's easy to imagine flow high on a rock face. But what about sitting at a desk? Flow can be found there too. When asked about the secret to his prolific career as an author, John Irving had this to offer: "The unspoken factor is love. The reason I can work so hard at my writing is that it's not work for me."

Irving is describing what it's like to be in a decades-long flow channel.

Breaking out of long-relied-on ways of operating is difficult, energy-consuming work for individuals, for teams, and for companies. Being in a flow channel allows us to maintain high levels of energy and confidence and enough love for a challenge to make risk-taking possible and worthwhile.

Flow channels aren't just desirable—they're achievable because there's nothing esoteric about getting into one, though of course it can take some serious work. Make sure you have a clear goal, then examine the challenge you face in comparison to the skills you have. Tune them to match, and you're likely to get into a state where you're ready to be far more flexible in your thinking.

In a state of flow, even if the work itself isn't of epic importance, intrinsic motivation can pour forth as from a fountain. Remember, intrinsic motivation means we enjoy the journey; we're not just looking forward to the destination. And flow makes the journey exciting. But if the challenge starts to exceed the individual's or team's skills, anxiety arises. Before long, the journey stops being enjoyable for its own sake. Attentional focus begins to shift, or is intentionally shifted by anxious managers who want to see immediate results, and we begin looking for external reasons to complete the challenge. Because we fall out of (or never achieve) flow at work, it can often feel like a grind. But we don't need to quit our jobs and risk our lives on a river to regain it. We simply need to find or return to our flow channel.

So how do we find our way to flow? How do we know when we're in it? And what can we do when we drift out of it?

Navigating Your Way to Flow

Create the Conditions

Finding flow, for ourselves as individuals and for our teams, begins by setting the stage. Recall that flow occurs when three conditions are present:

- We know what our goals are.

- We're able to get enough feedback from the environment to know that we're succeeding.

- Our level of skill is at or just below our level of challenge. In other words, we know how to do what needs to be done, but it's far from easy.

Throughout the act of creation, we can achieve and stay in flow by checking in regularly to assess our answers to these three questions:

Do I (or we) know what success really looks like? Too often, especially in creative endeavors, success is vaguely defined, and what definition there is isn't clearly shared among the team. Flow theory asks us to take the time to be very specific about what our targets are and how we'll know we're achieving them. We know what it means to get to the top of a rock face, but do our projects have similarly defined endpoints and markers along the way to let us know we're getting closer? If we're seeking flow, they should.

Can we get regular feedback to know if we're making progress? Wait, you may object, isn't getting positive feedback a creativity-killing grasping for approval and reward? It depends on how you treat feedback. If we undertake a project because we want a pat on the back from our boss or gasps of approval from our Twitter followers, then yes, we're unlikely to find flow. But if we receive feedback with a sense of unattached curiosity (positive feedback is a great sign we're making progress; negative feedback is a great chance to learn), we're increasing our chances to create flow. Treat feedback this way and it becomes a synergistic extrinsic motivator. Some projects take months or years before clear feedback is possible, but most don't have to. Take on the creative challenge of finding ways to build in more feedback more often and approach it all with open-minded curiosity.

Do we have the skills to match this challenge? It turns out that we humans are pretty awful judges of our own skills. Underskilled individuals tend to overestimate their abilities, while the highly skilled among us tend to be overly harsh in their self-judgment. The truth is, we don't really know for sure if we have the skills until we put them into action (we'll get to measuring skills in a moment). Still, it makes sense to do the equivalent of an equipment check as we set off on our journey. We can begin by mapping out the phases of a project from first conception to execution and refinement. Then we can ask ourselves and our team members a few key questions that rarely get examined. For each phase, or even for each necessary task, do we believe we have the specific skills we need? Or will the challenge be too much of a stretch in spots? If we can identify those places ahead of time, we can plan for them. What new skills or resources might we need in those moments of extra challenge to avoid falling into an immediate state of confused anxiety? Do we need to build in time for extra training and exploration, or do we need to bring in outside expertise at these critical junctures to prevent our skill and challenge levels from falling out of balance? A simple *flow map*, a step-by-step project plan that describes what we need to do to stay in flow, can often be the key to a project's maintaining its creative, risk-embracing edge and not falling into a motivation-less rut.

Measure Regularly

Asking these three simple questions (Do we know what success looks like? Can we get regular feedback? Do we have the skills we need?) and making adjustments so that we can answer yes to all of them makes the energetic state of flow possible. Of course, that's not enough. Next, we can begin to observe when we're in flow and when we're falling into anxiety or boredom. When Csikszentmihalyi first began his investigation, he observed that while many people reported a common experience of focus and love for their work, getting an accurate assessment of exactly when these moments happened or why was very difficult. He solved this problem by giving pagers to participants in one of his early studies. Every few hours, the pagers would buzz, and his subjects would write down what they were doing and then rank on a scale of one to ten their perceived concentration, involvement, and enjoyment. The method proved extremely effective for discovering people's propensity for flow and also the conditions that bring it about.

Fortunately, we don't need to carry a pager to put ourselves or our teams through Csikszentmihalyi's awareness-inducing regimen. We can simply set an hourly timer, and when it goes off, we can score ourselves in terms of concentration, involvement, and enjoyment.

What do we do if we find we're not in flow when we need focus and flexible thinking most? There is likely an imbalance between our perceived level of challenge and skill. Instead of continuing to attack the problem in a state of anxiety or boredom, we should step back and rebalance.

Tuning Up Skills

As we achieve more, more complex challenges will come our way, and that means we must inevitably, at times, pause and get back into a learning mode. Increasing our skills, especially in a field in which we've achieved a reasonable level of mastery, can seem like a daunting task, but there's a proven way to do it. It's called deliberate practice.

For a long time, psychologists have known that skill acquisition tends to follow a consistent pattern. When we're first trying to learn something new, like a foreign language, for instance, we're in the *cognitive phase.* Here we know we're beginners, we make endless mistakes, and we approach the challenge with a sort of nervous excitement. As we make progress and get more comfortable, we gradually progress to the *automatic phase.* Now we're in our comfort zone, so in the case of learning a language, we can speak it as if on autopilot. At this point, mediocre second-language speakers will often call themselves "fluent" because they can have conversations and navigate a busy day abroad without much conscious thought. But their accents might still suck, and their comprehension might be more like a third grader's than an adult's. Still, "fluent" seems like a good enough goal, and many stop trying nearly as hard to improve. They've reached what journalist Joshua Foer has called the "OK Plateau."

But what if, after a few years of fluently speaking a language, we're asked to translate a complicated document? We need to make rapid and significant improvement. Studies of those who transcend the OK Plateau show that these individuals almost universally engage in deliberate practice. By laser-focusing on the parts of the skill they're not yet great at, they force their minds back into the rapid-growth cognitive phase. Great musicians don't spend all day practicing the songs they've mastered, though pretty good musicians do. They focus on the piece that bedevils them and stick with it until they've nailed it. They note their inevitable mistakes and intentionally mark their improvements.

When we fall out of flow and want to tune up our skills, we need to step back from the challenge we're engaged in for a little while each day to work on the specific things we haven't much improved on in quite some time. Deliberate practice means setting aside about an hour at a time to focus on one weakness (more than an hour has been shown to produce burnout) and repeatedly practice improving it. Forcing ourselves out of autopilot and back into a cognitive state will rapidly tune our skills up. As we make progress, we can return to the larger challenge we're trying to surmount with a much better chance of getting back into flow.

Tune Down the Challenge

We can also calibrate our match of skills and challenge by reducing the degree of difficulty of the task we're tackling. I recently spoke with a brilliant executive who was working on her public speaking. She was stuck because she had defined her challenge as "creating a talk that nobody else has ever given that will change my listeners' lives." This was a noble goal, but it was producing tremendous anxiety. The goal was enormously ambitious, fuzzy, and difficult to measure. Fortunately, she decided to reframe the first step of the challenge as "discovering what I know that I think my audiences would benefit from hearing." She was able to get started, and before long she found herself in a state of focused creativity. Tuning down a challenge doesn't have to mean tuning down ambition. It can mean breaking the objective down into smaller, more achievable pieces. Or it might mean deleting goals that have slipped into the challenge definition that are extremely difficult but aren't critical to success. While a talk that "nobody else has ever given" is a nice goal, it has little to do with whether the presentation will be useful, entertaining, and informative. And these conditions are far more relevant to her success as a public speaker.

Outsmarting Dings and Chimes

If flow offers us energy and an ability to take risks, it also demands a certain amount of focus, and focus is a quality in increasingly short supply today.

"Anyone who has experienced flow knows that the deep enjoyment it provides requires an equal degree of disciplined concentration," Csikszentmihalyi wrote in 1990. Even then, he was concerned about the effects of television and digital entertainment on our ability to maintain flow. A quarter century later, the demands on our attention have multiplied to a degree he could hardly have imagined, and they're becoming increasingly alluring. Here's where McLeay and his team, alone in the wilderness, had an advantage over those of us who work within the range of Wi-Fi and cell towers. We now live in a world of constant distraction. Mastering distraction and even harnessing certain kinds of it to our advantage have become critical skills in maintaining the energy needed to break with our comfortable but no longer useful ways.

Let's look again at what awaits us when we are chronically out of flow: anxiety or boredom. Sitting with these uncomfortable emotions is difficult, and our minds will look for nearly any way out. A 2014 study at the University of Virginia asked participants to sit quietly with their thoughts for fifteen minutes. Their one distraction: severe static shocks that were painful but not dangerous. Most of the participants chose the shock over uninterrupted quiet contemplation. If boredom is uncomfortable, anxiety is even less desirable. Of course, the most productive way out of anxiety or boredom is to do the deliberate work of returning to flow by adjusting our challenges and skills. But that takes concentration and discipline. An easier way out is simply to place our attention on something more satisfying. And those somethings are everywhere.

On average we check our email fifteen times and our phones forty-six times per day. A recent study found that Millennials, who check their phones on average eighty-five times a day, are more forgetful than people over fifty-five, a possible first-in-history role reversal between young and old. Ironically for Csikszentmihalyi, who's so concerned about distraction, mobile game creators have built on his findings to create casual games, available in three-minute spurts on a smartphone, designed to produce flow. As a player reaches new levels of mastery, the level of challenge inches up too. As I've written this book, a task that has often brought me into flow but has also occasionally driven me to despair, I've often had to resist the temptation to play such games, which I discovered while researching flow. They are enormously enjoyable and absorbing. Of course, they do little to help anyone achieve goals.

How deadly is the problem of distraction for business? Recent estimates put the cost to the US economy of time spent on social media sites at work at $650 billion annually. An average worker costs his or her company more than $4,500 a year in productivity thanks to digital distraction. A full 10 percent of the US workforce spends more time on social media while at the office than they do working.

The good news is that simple awareness of the perils of distraction can go a long way to giving us advantages over it.

A few years back, two researchers at Carnegie Mellon, Alessandro Acquisti and Eyal Peer, decided to study whether there was a simple way to protect people from distraction's worst effects. They ran an experiment in which participants read a short amount of text and then responded to some questions to see if they understood what they had read. Participants were divided into three groups. One group was simply told to read the text and answer the questions. The other two groups were told that at any moment they might be given further instructions via instant message. These two groups were texted twice while they were reading. The effect on their performance was sobering. The interrupted groups answered incorrectly 20 percent more often. In fact, as the New York Times journalist who covered the study pointed out, the distractions were "enough to turn a B-minus student (80 percent) into a failure (62 percent)." But that's not the end of the story.

In a second round of the experiment, the two groups were again told that distractions might be coming; one received texts, but the other didn't. Surprisingly, the performance of this last group, which was prepared for an interruption that didn't come, improved by 43 percent—pushing it above that of participants who were never interrupted at all. The researchers attributed the improvement to increased vigilance, arguing that being aware of the possibility of interruptions but successfully avoiding them may ratchet up our focus even beyond the baseline of no distractions at all.

What can we learn from this? When we hope to move into a state of flow, we'd do well to create a "cone of focus." This is a special condition in which we make an agreement with ourselves or others to stay on target for a set amount of time. We can do this by naming the most unhelpful distractions we're likely to face along with simple strategies to avoid them. For example, "We tend to get a lot of customer texts around lunch. Let's all agree to put an autoresponder on and get back to them at one o'clock." In a group setting, a shared distraction list can instantly create social norms that stop digital pitfalls like email checking and instant messaging in their tracks. Such lists sound simple, but by acknowledging random distractors for what they are—unhelpful activities that decrease our performance—we can both vastly decrease their power and turn on a subtle cognitive program that increases vigilance and attentional control.

Of course a simple step like establishing a cone of focus isn't a panacea in a world of constant digital distraction. For some who rely on flow, finding a cone of focus requires more extreme measures. "What you have to do," explains author Jonathan Franzen, describing how he's blocked his antiquated laptop from accessing the internet, "is you plug in an Ethernet cable with superglue, and you saw off the little head of it." He's done this after removing his wireless card, altering his operating system to remove preinstalled games and alerts, and placing himself and his laptop in a rented office stripped of any visual stimulation.

Franzen can't take any chances—his writing process demands enormous energy and concentration. He writes six or seven days a week, all day, beginning at 7 a.m. He speaks his dialog aloud as he writes, often winding up hoarse by the end of a session. His pace and concentration are extreme, but they have allowed him to become one of the world's most celebrated writers of fiction.

The Good Side of Distraction

Of course, there's a time for letting our minds wander, and distraction, like extrinsic motivation, isn't a universally bad thing. I'm sure you're familiar with the phenomenon that many great ideas come at unexpected moments when you're not consciously thinking of the problem you're working on, such as in the shower or on a run. Research has shown that the most effective way to solve a creative problem is, in fact, to concentrate on it with deep focus for a limited period and then to free your mind to do some unstructured thinking about other things, returning to a concentrated focus if a creative solution still has not presented itself.

Scott Barry Kaufman, scientific director of the Imagination Institute at the University of Pennsylvania, told me, "It's helpful to take your mind away from a difficult task." But he warned that there's an art to intentionally relaxing our focus. "You need to engage in something that's not mindless but offers a different kind of mindful engagement." He advises that we should remind ourselves to stay goal driven, even as we let our attention roam, rather than mindlessly throwing our attention at whatever comes before us, whether that is the chime of a phone or a conversation we overhear or a string of email messages.

When I asked Mihaly Csikszentmihalyi if there was a place for distraction in his model of flow, he told me that Leonardo da Vinci would wander the streets of Venice looking at peeling paint patterns, letting them rattle around in his brain, and that would help him think of new painting techniques. Csikszentmihalyi says, "Lowering your focus can be useful if you have a very clear problem to work on; it can give you a different perspective." The key is that we are mindfully relaxing our attention, and this allows us to benefit from unconscious consideration of the problem. That's not the same thing as compulsively checking in with our phones, though these open and quiet moments are easily overcome by the urge to reconnect to the endless flow of digital information. We throw away these moments at our creative peril.

Ascend the Nile Expedition Day 30

The Ascend the Nile team is traveling through the dreaded Sudd in their little Zap Cats. The Sudd is the world's largest swamp, and the Nile flows into it in South Sudan. In the rainy season it can swell to the size of England. To the untrained eye, the swamp looks like a dense forest of reeds that in places grow up to three times the height of a man.

The team's GPS has failed, and the swamp has swallowed up the river current. The direction from which the river flows and, therefore, in which the team needs to head, is indiscernible. Often channels that look like roadways among the reeds appear. Each offers hope of safe passage. Most will dead-end after many miles of commitment. Heading up the wrong channel could cost the explorers hours and gallons of precious gasoline. To their left and right, vegetation towers over their heads. Their fuel is dwindling. What's more, they cannot be spotted from the air. A rescue is almost surely impossible.

They are nervous. But they are also observant. They notice that large clumps of hyacinths are floating about freely. The invasive plants grow on the surface of the water, without roots tethering them to the swamp's floor. The team members note a direction to their movement—the hyacinths are subtly following the river's current. They steer against the grain of the traveling flowers through the maze of channels and at last emerge to the glorious sight of the shimmering expanse of the Nile stretching out before them.

Why were Cam McLeay and his team able to repeatedly overcome the seemingly impossible in their quixotic search for the source of the Nile, when so many other teams and individuals resign themselves to the mediocre in situations far more consequential for their careers, their customers, and humanity at large?

Was it luck? It could have been if they had overcome just one or two obstacles. But dozens? Not likely. Superior skills? These guys were good, but time and again they found themselves in way over their heads. What really distinguishes the Ascend the Nile team is their ability to remain in flow. They had a clear goal and could measure their progress. They found a challenge just beyond their considerable skills. Far removed from our modern world of distraction, they stayed clearheaded and focused. As a result they experienced love for what they were doing and found the energy to overcome every obstacle. While few of us aspire to be river explorers, who wouldn't want to face danger and challenge with this level of joy and ingenuity?

Inspired as I was by Cam McLeay's flexibility of thinking and spirit of adventure, something about him troubled me. He was incongruous. His face, deeply lined by countless hours in the sun, made him appear late middle-aged, while his voice burst forth with the rapid enthusiasm of a teenager talking about a favorite sport. The effect of a child's spirit in a man's body was charming, but his Nile expedition had been no sport. Along the way, rebel soldiers killed one of his team members in the bush; another miraculously survived being shot in the head. They had faced death half a dozen other times, all in pursuit of a dream with only symbolic meaning.

"It gives you a reason to live," McLeay said of his explorations. There is no doubt he fits the model of an unsafe thinker, but is he a role model for the rest of us? Is his ability to innovate and take risks mostly the result of having found something he is so passionate about that he is happily willing to die for it? And is that an impossible standard for the rest of us who don't necessarily feel a deep love for every challenge we engage in?

I asked Csikszentmihalyi this question, and he told me that getting into flow can make even mundane tasks motivating and release creative thinking. If you fall in love with the process of creation, he said, you can apply it almost anywhere (though he did admit, rather specifically, that he would never be motivated to solve trigonometry problems). I tend to agree, but the word "almost" is important. We can invigorate ourselves by understanding the basic principles of focus and motivation within our current situations. We can tune challenges up and down and introduce motivational synergy to keep us alive and alert throughout. And we can solve the problems presented to us even if they don't represent our life's purpose. But there are limits. At times, our work may present difficult challenges that just don't align with our deeper purpose and may even run up against it. These challenges will never motivate us to step out of safety, and failing to recognize when it's time to walk away can lead to years of frustration and psychic pain.

E. Paul Torrance, who studied creativity his entire professional life and published more than 1,800 papers on the subject, gives perhaps the clearest advice on how to both find passion in the challenges we face and admit to ourselves when it's time to turn away from them. He boiled his research down to four simple rules:

1. Don't be afraid to fall in love with something and pursue it with intensity and depth.
2. Know, understand, take pride in, practice, develop, use, exploit, and enjoy your greatest strengths.
3. Learn to free yourself from the expectations of others and to walk away from the games that others try to impose upon you. Free yourself to "play your own game" in such a way as to make good use of your gifts.
4. Don't waste a lot of expensive energy in trying to do things for which you have little ability or love.

In other words, we can find the motivation that drives creative breakthrough in anything we do. We need not drop everything and head for our nearest river. On the other hand, if what we're doing has lost meaning, we will find ourselves always at a disadvantage in finding our flow.

MOTIVATION: KEY TAKEAWAYS

Use motivational synergy to stay energized

Focus yourself and your team primarily on intrinsic motivation, or love of what you're doing. That's where your deepest source of creative energy comes from. But extrinsic rewards, as long as they don't feel manipulative or coercive, can help you and those you lead get through the inevitable slog that comes with creation. Most of us are like Julie Wainwright, motivated by a love of what we do but also driven by a desire for some mix of wealth, recognition, and impact. That's OK, if we manage it well.

When it's time to dream big and imagine, keep the extrinsic incentives away. When it's time to refine and grind out an execution, a little friendly competition, low-level prizes, and creative rewards can work wonders.

Put yourself in flow

Remember that flow occurs when we know what we are trying to achieve, our skills are up to or just below our level of challenge, and we're getting regular feedback. Do this and you'll find a consistent source of intrinsic motivation, even if you're in an office park rather than on a river.

How can you ensure that markers of success are clear and carefully measured along the way? Do you regularly engage in deliberate practice (focusing on improving where you're weak) to keep your skills growing as your level of challenge grows? When the going gets tough, are you willing to tone down your level of challenge until you're back in flow?

Make distraction work for you

We can't create breakthroughs by staying maniacally focused at all times. But mindless distraction is one of the most powerful creativity killers that we confront. Walking the streets of Venice with a soft focus like da Vinci can work wonders, but that's not the same thing as obsessively playing Words with Friends.

Recall the study in which those who were aware of the possibility of distraction but avoided it boosted their performance. How can you become more mindful of what pulls you out of concentration and create a "cone of focus" to protect yourself? And how can you build in even half an hour a day to let your mind wander, without a device in hand?

PART 3

LEARNING

CHAPTER 5

The Explorer's Edge

How to pursue expertise
without falling into the expert's trap

You step into the exam room. There's a quiet buzz as your classmates settle in around you. You confidently walk up to your desk, sit down, and turn over the paper in front of you. The first question stops you cold. "What were the erinaceous characteristics of senior British officials before the German invasion of Czechoslovakia?" You squint and hunch down to look at the paper more closely. Is "erinaceous" a word? Are you expected to know what it means? You skip to the second question, which asks you to identify the various percussive instruments that comprise the Javanese gamelan. You vaguely remember having seen a gamelan concert a decade ago, but had this been part of the course work? The third question is written in a pictographic language you've never seen before. What's going on? You remember in a flash that you've forgotten to study for this exam. In fact, you haven't been going to class for the last six weeks. You begin to panic. Then you wake up.

Being unprepared for an exam is one of the most common nightmares people experience, and that holds across cultures. Stepping into a high-stakes situation without being ready is terrifying for nearly everyone. In fact, dream researcher Tony Zadra says this nightmare is not just experienced by those who go through life truly underprepared but is particularly common among the highly educated and successful.

So many experience the dream so often that researchers have tried to identify an adaptive function for it. Why would this nightmare be so common if it were just a painful annoyance? Dream researcher David Fontana believes the exam nightmare may be a protective warning from our psyches, a taste of what awaits us if we choose not to invest in building up enough expertise to tackle life's challenges. Such dreams, he says, "encourage the dreamer to face up to the shortcomings that he or she may otherwise have been unwilling to see."

For years, I was one of the unfortunate many who experienced the exam nightmare fairly regularly. Despite the dire warnings it carried, however, I always found a pleasant aspect to the experience. The dream itself was awful, but as soon as I awoke, I would remember that I had finished school long ago and held a job in which I thought I pretty much knew what I was doing. In these moments, I experienced a sense of sweet relief.

We have such a deep-seated fear of not knowing, or being exposed as not knowing, that we experience it as a species-wide nightmare, while we find enormous comfort in contemplating our own expertise.

It's true that we delight in pointing out how foolish experts can appear when they confidently predict the transportation dominance of the flying car or the Segway, tell us smoking is good for us, fail to anticipate the housing crash of 2007, or confidently read a Hillary Clinton victory in the 2016 polling data. Still, we are right to fear not having expertise when we need it. And we need it often. It's extremely difficult to create anything of value in a field without first becoming something of an expert. That's obviously the case in highly technical endeavors like sequencing a genome or repairing an airplane, but researchers have been emphatic that it's also the case for artists, business leaders, and inventors.

In her model of creativity, Teresa Amabile puts expertise front and center, naming what she calls "domain-relevant skills" as one of the four key components of effective creation. Herbert Simon, the Nobel Prize–winning psychologist and artificial intelligence pioneer, said that our knowledge, technical skills, and common problem-solving patterns, which we can only learn through study and apprenticeship, define our "network of possible wanderings." Simon's poetic image illustrates the fact that we can't effectively explore the unknown without a compass of expertise to guide us through it. Inventing the new, in Simon's view, comes first from understanding, then deconstructing and recombining, what is already known and understood.

At first, I found the emphasis on expertise as a prerequisite for creativity somewhat dispiriting. I've long wanted to believe in the concept of the naive newcomer, the novice who cares nothing for the rules of a field and shakes the world with a fresh insight. If that were the route to creative success, after all, we'd all be spared a lot of study and hard work. Unfortunately, there's scant evidence to indicate such dilettantes are particularly common or effective.

Why then, if expertise is so indispensable, do experts so often lead us astray? Why are experts so slow to update their views in the face of new evidence? And why do relative beginners sometimes beat experts at their own game? The answers to these questions are critical because, throughout the process of creation, we must constantly decide whether to rely on or question our expertise, to deepen what we know or seek entirely new ideas, to see the world through the eyes of the expert or the beginner. Searching for these answers, I found that there is no one right answer. But we can learn plenty to help us build our expertise without getting trapped by it.

Demystifying the Beginner's Advantage

Krtin Nithiyanandam had a hard time believing he had really come so far on Google searches, self-directed study, and borrowed equipment. He was only fifteen years old, a tenth grader, and unless he was missing something, he seemed to have invented a way to diagnose the onset of Alzheimer's disease ten years earlier than other detection systems. With no prior experience in medical research, he came upon the idea for his diagnostic tool by surfing the web.

"I usually play a lot of squash," he told me. "But then I fractured my hip pretty badly. I had a lot of time on my hands, so I started to explore more science." Science had always held an emotional appeal for Nithiyanandam. Without complex and leading-edge surgery, a childhood buildup of dead cells in his ears would have left him deaf. He still carries tiny implants to help him hear. To the young child, science had seemed like benevolent magic. To the young adult, it seemed like a playground for an active and curious mind clocking a lot of time on the couch.

Nithiyanandam's first thought was to find a disease that afflicted millions and then to do a little research to see if he could cure it. Why not? He chose Alzheimer's, and before long he came upon descriptions of antibodies able to cross the notoriously vigilant blood-brain barrier—and that gave him an idea. What if he could attach a fluorescent particle to such an antibody, a particle that would latch on to the proteins known to drive the early onset of the disease? (He had learned about this cause of Alzheimer's from Google as well.) Perhaps this would allow him to make a map of these dangerous proteins in the brain, determining their position and frequency in a patient who otherwise had no symptoms.

"My school doesn't have the kind of lab I'd need to do the project," he said. "And a lot of people didn't think the idea of a fifteen-year-old using expensive equipment and chemicals was a very good idea. I got a lot of no's."

But Nithiyanandam is the type of optimistic and energetic teenager whom the word "no" seems to bounce right off of. He next reached out to some local charities that support kids in science. The idea turned out to be so strong that he managed to raise about $150,000 to pursue it. Cambridge University offered to let him work on some of their equipment.

The first tests were enormously encouraging. Just as he'd hoped, Nithiyanandam's little Trojan horses were crossing the blood-brain barrier, attaching to the disease-causing proteins, and throwing up their flare signals. Maps of harmful proteins within the brain were beginning to form. His idea had worked!

But then the project took a turn for the worse. After a few days of glowing, the maps began to dissipate and then disappeared. He had no idea why.

"I was a bit annoyed," Nithiyanandam admits about watching his project potentially go up in smoke. But he also says that because he wasn't a professor with a reputation and career to defend, he didn't panic.

He kept at it, continuing to create more of his little machines, closely observing them as the glow began to dim. Then one day he discovered what had been going on. He caught one of his creations behaving more like a bomb than a flare. It was destroying the toxic protein it had attached itself to. His machines weren't failing; they were actually attacking the cause of the disease. Nithiyanandam had invented not only a detection system but also an enormously promising line of treatment for what has been a mostly untreatable affliction. For his work he would win the 2015 Scientific American Innovator Award.

Nithiyanandam says that while he made some refinements to previous researchers' work, he didn't invent anything new. Other scientists had discovered the antibodies, the fluorescent particles, and the toxic proteins. They'd even tried to develop a cure with a couple of these ingredients, but the early results hadn't been promising. So they'd left the whole approach for dead.

"My breakthrough isn't based on a lot of new stuff," Nithiyanandam told me. "You just have to remember that things that are thought to work one way, sometimes work another."

He's emphatic that he couldn't have gotten anywhere if he'd tried his project fifteen years earlier, before so much science became open source and available online. He was pulling from an enormous body of expertise developed by other scientists. He just hadn't also pulled the information that the approach he was trying was likely to fail.

The beginner's advantage is well known in the sciences, and it tends to follow a certain pattern. An innovator will spend up to age eighteen getting a basic education and up to about age thirty learning the specifics of his or her field. Next comes a couple years on the job and then voilà—a breakthrough. That's how the authors of a recent survey of Nobel Prize winners explained the huge concentration of laureates who did their prize-worthy work in their thirties. The average age was thirty-six. Why only a couple of years in the field? The authors look at it this way: "The most important conceptual work typically involves radical departures from existing paradigms, and the ability to identify and appreciate these radical departures may be greatest shortly after initial exposure to a paradigm, before it has been fully assimilated."

With this in mind, Nithiyanandam's story becomes less unlikely. Remarkably, he condensed his education phase, thanks to Google and an obviously sharp mind, from a couple decades into several months. "I had an initial idea which was incredibly bare bones, ludicrously simple," he says. From there, he tapped professional researchers to refine the details. He accessed all he needed to know without getting bogged down in the existing (mistaken) knowledge that his idea would not work. Nithiyanandam, like the young Nobel Prize winners, was a relative beginner, but he was far from a dilettante. He did everything he could to absorb the key knowledge of his field but never got so immersed in it that he lost his fresh perspective. He became enough of an expert to know what he was doing but was enough of an outsider to avoid exposure to a piece of mistaken conventional wisdom that, had he absorbed it, he admits, would have ended his search.

But is exposure to bad information the only disadvantage experts face compared to beginners? Or is there danger in accumulating good information too? It turns out there is.

Rice University researcher Erik Dane uses the word "entrenchment" for the trap that experts must inevitably contend with. Past a certain point of expertise, the more we learn, build confidence, and achieve authority, the less sensitive we risk becoming to the signals and possibilities in our environment. Yes, Dane told me, you do need to build up an expert's understanding of your field before you can generate radical and useful ideas. But he draws an inverted U to describe the relationship between expertise and radical creativity.

Gaining enough knowledge to understand a field gets us to the top of the U, Dane contends. Here we are most able to contribute new, important insights. (This is where Nithiyanandam likely found himself

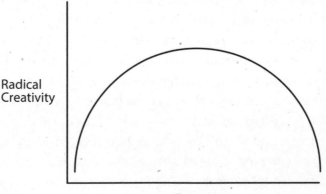

when discovering his Alzheimer's cure.) Unfortunately, many experts, after reaching this high point, slide down the other end toward a fixed, inflexible way of seeing the world. Not only do they become frozen in their thinking, but they often, inadvertently, use their positions of power to freeze a whole discipline. Sigmund Freud, who both pioneered the field of psychology and then wrapped it in a thick orthodoxy, probably had slid down the entrenchment side of the *U* when he wrote in *Civilization and Its Discontents*, "The conceptions I have summarized here I first put forward only tentatively, but in the course of time they have won such a hold over me that I can no longer think in any other way."

Seeing So Clearly We Become Blind

Experts don't just process problems more effectively; within their realm of expertise, they actually see the world differently than beginners. Consider how a chess grandmaster and a beginning player see the pieces on a board. The beginner might be able to read the positions of pieces and think a couple moves ahead, eliminating the illegal moves easily and then the clearly stupid ones. But the rest of the possibilities? Well, they provide a lot of information without a lot of meaning. Considering all possibilities could literally take weeks.

Decision-making researcher Gary Klein says that the grandmaster sees an entirely different board. Where the beginner sees noise, the master sees patterns and meaning. In fact, grandmasters can simply glance at a board and later recall the exact location of each piece (interestingly they cannot do this better than a novice if the pieces are arranged in a meaningless way). Reading the board, the grandmaster can dismiss thousands of suboptimal possibilities based on patterns he isn't even consciously aware he's recognizing. This allows the grandmaster to focus, considering only the best moves, while the beginner, overwhelmed by the possibilities, easily falls prey to errors. The beginner doesn't stand a chance.

In our own fields of expertise, our brains work much like that of the grandmaster. The knowledge we accumulate is brilliantly organized. It has to be, or an abundance of knowledge would simply be a curse. Studies since the 1950s have shown that people in possession of large amounts of unstructured information are slower to search through and recall knowledge. Too much information tends to gunk up the mental works. Experts, however, manage to solve this problem; they are not slower or less able to recall important stuff. In fact, they tend to be very fast and efficient. That's because their brains have neatly sorted individual facts and ideas into complex, interrelated networks. You can imagine these networks as like a library. A library contains tens of thousands of books, each containing hundreds or thousands of ideas. Randomly arranged in piles, these ideas would be useless. But you can walk into a library and, often within minutes (even before the invention of computerized search), retrieve the exact information you are looking for because each book is catalogued and shelved according to a precise system. The network of an expert's brain works on very similar principles of organization and association.

Once the foundations and rules of a network have been laid down, it's not hard to add new bits of information into it. There's a ready-made place for everything: romance, mystery, science, folklore, cookbooks. The more we use the network, the more comfortable with it we grow, and the easier it is to integrate novel information into familiar categories.

The problem is that while our ability to process the information we've stored is enhanced, our thinking also becomes more rigid. Klein points out that while expertise can make us enormously efficient at playing an established game, it can also make us slower to realize when the game has changed and less able to respond to those changes. For example, expert bridge players have been shown to have more trouble than novices in adapting when important rules, like who gets to lead, are suddenly tweaked. Our expert's mind, so used to moving quickly and efficiently, tries to fit new information into old boxes so it can use its rapid processing power. "Oh, that's just a new flavor of an old problem," our expert brain says. Too often it's not. After all, most of the problems we face in a world of rapid change have little in common with a two-dimensional chessboard with rules that never change.

Yes, the mental mapping and cataloging we do as we develop expertise allow us to sort through information at enormous speed and quickly rule out possibilities that would be a waste of time. But as powerful as this mental mapping can be, it's often overly seductive. It can lead us to overperceive patterns and apply them when we shouldn't, and that is how, even with an expert's mind full of good information, we can still make terrible expert judgments.

In 1983, Philip Tetlock wanted to see just how accurate experts tended to be. So he chose 284 people who made their living as pundits. He asked them, year after year, to predict the likelihood of various large changes happening around the world in the near·future—revolutions, wars, political movements. By the time he wrapped up his study in 2003 and the predictions had proven right or wrong, he had collected 82,361 forecasts. Along the way he amassed a lot of data about how the experts made their predictions and how confident they were of them.

So how did Tetlock's experts do? Terribly. If he had simply blind-folded these people and had them throw darts at various predictions, they would have done better. In the aggregate, all their studying, rea-soning, and analysis not only didn't help but actually decreased the like-lihood that they would be right.

How can that be? It seems that one would have to consciously try to predict badly to perform worse than chance. Tetlock explained his findings, in large part, by reference to experts' overactive pattern rec-ognition. To illustrate this foible of human psychology, Tetlock recalls an experiment he observed decades earlier at Yale University, in which a rat made its way through a simple maze. There was only one decision to make—go right or left—and the rat was repeatedly allowed to run through the maze in search of food. The food was placed down one path or another in an apparently random fashion but actually according to an algorithm that ensured its placement on the left side 60 percent of the time. The rat wasn't the only one being tested. A group of students was brought in to make their own predictions. At first, both the rat and the students guessed right about 50 percent of the time, which is exactly what you'd expect from chance if you didn't know the placement of the food was rigged. But over time, the results began to diverge. Before long, the rat nearly always went left, giving it about a 60 percent success rate. It was learning. The Ivy League students, on the other hand, weren't and continued to be wrong almost 50 percent of the time. The rat had them beat by a significant margin.

Tetlock thought he knew why. The students couldn't help imagin-ing that they were figuring out a significant underlying pattern—that as high-achieving intellectuals, they could see into the minds of the researchers and figure out the trick. "We insist on looking for order in random sequences . . . like 'food appears in alternating two left/one right sequences, except after the third cycle when food pops up on the right,'" Tetlock explains. The students would create a theory and over-weight supportive evidence for it while discounting counterevidence. They were crafting, as humans do, a story about their own intelligence and ability to see meaning. The meaning they saw, however, was wrong, and that's how the rat was able to beat them.

Now imagine taking this desire to find and invest heavily in patterns out into the real world. One group of experts Tetlock studied made the pattern-recognition error regarding predictions about military interventions. These military experts had invested in the idea, based on the US experience in Vietnam, that military interventions always end in quagmires. "The list includes Nicaragua, Haiti, Bosnia, Colombia, Afghanistan, and Iraq (all new American Vietnams), Afghanistan (the Soviet Union's Vietnam), Chechnya (Russia's Vietnam), Kashmir (India's Vietnam), Lebanon (Israel's Vietnam), Angola (Cuba's Vietnam), the Basque territory (Spain's Vietnam), Eritrea (Ethiopia's Vietnam), Northern Ireland (Britain's Vietnam), and Kampuchea (Vietnam's Vietnam)," Tetlock wrote.

Tetlock found that not only will some experts' knowledge networks consistently predict failure for military interventions, but the experts will explain away the failure of those predictions as a fluke. Then, in constructing the story that excuses this failure, they will often become further locked into their points of view. And that's how they managed to perform, consistently, worse than chance.

As we build and improve our expert knowledge networks, we gain not only a higher volume of information but far more complex connections between pieces of knowledge. The more exquisitely complex these knowledge networks become, the more useful and uniquely ours they become as well. But what happens when we encounter new information that breaks the schema of our network? If the network is barely developed, we can easily redesign it, greeting the new evidence as a welcome early signal that we had missed something and were heading down the wrong path. If the network is richly developed and we have invested heavily in it over time, that's not so easy. Changing it will take an enormous amount of disentangling. So what happens to the new information that doesn't fit? It gets forced into a box where it doesn't belong. Or it simply gets ignored, while our knowledge networks become more rigid. It happens to all of us. It's just part of being human.

From Expert to Explorer

We need expertise. But in gaining it, we inevitably face the expert's trap. So are we destined to slide down the wrong end of Erik Dane's inverted *U*? Not necessarily. Dane says one of the most effective things we can do is put ourselves in situations where we're novices. Get out more and explore. It's a key way, he says, of taking the rigidity out of overdeveloped knowledge networks.

Recent evidence indicates that time spent in the unfamiliar can enhance anyone's creativity significantly. For example, one recent experiment put a new spin on a very old creativity challenge known as the Duncker candle problem. In this classic puzzle, participants must figure out a way to attach a candle to a wall using only a pack of matches and a box of tacks. This is one of those confounding tasks that preys upon fixed knowledge networks. Our brain sees the tacks as a fastener, the matches as a tool for melting wax, and the cardboard box that holds the tacks as irrelevant. The key to solving this problem, however, is the irrelevant-seeming box. One must empty the box, attach the bottom of the candle to it with melted wax, and then tack the candle-box assembly to the wall.

In a 2007 version of this experiment, researchers divided participants into two groups: those who had spent significant time living abroad and those who hadn't. The difference was impressive. Those with multicultural experience solved the puzzle 60 percent of the time; those without it, only 42 percent of the time.

How can we explain this wide performance gap? Living abroad presents a major challenge to our entrenched mental models of how the world works. When you arrive in an unfamiliar culture, you simply cannot categorize all new information along old patterns. Familiar objects have unexpected new meanings and uses. Strange-seeming ideas are widely embraced and made useful in ways you never could have predicted.

Familiar routines are interrupted. You have two choices: either maintain your expert mind-set by trying to fit all this information into existing knowledge networks, wildly distorting reality in the process, or loosen those networks, recognizing that they are but one model of the world. The American writer Gertrude Stein, who did her most creative work while living in Paris, famously described getting out of your domain of comfort as a prerequisite for creativity: "Writers have to have two countries, the one where they belong and the one in which they live really."

Even if moving to another country isn't practical, immersion in any pursuit outside your comfort zone can loosen your attachment to a single mode of processing new information and put your inner expert in check. Tetlock, the expert on experts, found this to be true with his predictors. He divided his experts into two species: hedgehogs, who "know a lot about one great thing," and foxes, who "know a bit about many things." Foxes who displayed curiosity across domains, even those in which they were not expert, were far more reliable in their predictions (though still far more fallible than we might hope our experts to be).

Stepping out of our domain of expertise is risky. It's hard to know if the foray will ultimately pay off in direct and measurable ways—if we will effectively combine new information with old to make something greater than the sum of its parts. At the same time, this level of risk keeps your colleagues and competitors from venturing into unexplored territory and explains why the opportunity for invention is so high. Taking that step into the unknown allowed architect Mick Pearce to create one of the most sustainable buildings in the world.

Pearce liked to get out from behind his desk to indulge his seemingly bizarre, amateur's fascination with termites. The tiny creatures, Pearce observed, without central planning or control and with brains the size of a pinhead, managed to create skyscrapers that, relative to their body size, are the tallest built structures in the world. If termites were scaled up to the size of humans, their mounds would be nearly a mile high. Pearce began to wonder what they might know that human architects didn't.

Indulging his curiosity and turning amateur entomologist, Pearce discovered an even more complex termite talent than building vertically. The insects he studied lived on a special fungus that only grows at thirty degrees Celsius. Though the desert temperatures outside their mounds swing wildly each day by up to forty degrees, the termites manage to cultivate their crop at a constant and perfect temperature.

The secret is proper ventilation. The colonies create channels that conduct air from vents at the bottom to vents at the top. As temperatures change throughout the day, the termites open and close these vents to optimize airflow. Needless to say, the whole system requires no outside source of energy.

Pearce became convinced that he could copy the termites' strategy on a human scale, and in 1996, he got his chance. Asked to design an office building in Zimbabwe's capital city of Harare, he decided to draw on his study of termites.

The building he designed features a complex, interdependent system of ventilation, overhangs that provide shade, and strategic glazing, all inspired by his insect role models. The payoff was enormous. Pearce's Eastgate Centre requires less than 10 percent of the energy of the glass-block buildings built all around it, saving its owners $3.5 million right away on the air-conditioning system they never had to install, not to mention the enormous savings on energy use and maintenance over the next decades of operation.

"The buildings I do are a strange concoction of biomimicry, which is the process of copying nature," Pearce says of his work. And while his wanderings out of his field are unique and seemingly bizarre, his solutions tend to work because they are, like the natural world, elegantly efficient. That means that they are ultimately less risky than more mainstream innovation. "Eastgate is based on a primitive and simplistic idea," he says of its success.

Studies of creative genius have long highlighted the power of bringing disparate fields together. Albert Einstein fueled his creative insights in the sciences by passionately playing classical music at an amateur level. Oprah Winfrey went from local talk show host to a figure many regard as the most influential woman in the world by constantly adding one personal passion after the next to her empire—from literature to film to spirituality.

Pushing ourselves to spend less time as experts and more time as explorers loosens overly rigid knowledge networks and gives us a personal edge as thinkers and creators. But the practice doesn't only work at the individual level. Introducing a single explorer to a team of experts can have stunning and immediate results, as it did for the US Navy during World War II.

∞∞∞∞∞∞∞

Abraham Wald's colleagues, in every job he held, knew him as a genius. Born in the Austro-Hungarian empire in 1902, he showed enormous promise as a mathematician at an early age. But the early twentieth century was a terrible time to be a European Jew trying to establish himself in academia. Denied a teaching position by the Nazi regime in Austria and eventually fearing for his life, Wald fled to the United States, where his talents were immediately recognized. He would soon pioneer new, if somewhat arcane to the public, thinking in statistical analysis, geometry, and economic theory. But his work on airplanes, a field he knew nothing about, would be his most celebrated contribution to his adopted country.

By the early 1940s, the Allies were suffering maddening losses of their bombers to Axis artillery fire. Despite a superior ability to manufacture planes and train pilots, the Allies were throwing the advantage away as aircraft were being shot down multiple times daily. So the US Navy decided to turn to outsiders for new solutions to this expensive, deadly, and seemingly intractable problem.

Fortunately, they knew exactly where to look. The Statistical Research Group, located a block from Columbia University in Manhattan, was an ingenious program to bring statisticians into the war effort. The men assembled there were considered the leading lights in their field, though they worked in abstraction and theory. They could sling a slide ruler at dizzying speeds but would have been stumped by a rifle. The navy thought these outsiders would have an advantage where their own experts got stymied. Wald, regarded as the finest mind in the group, was invited to offer his perspective.

As Wald joined the team reviewing the problem, the dominant proposal already on the table was straightforward. The Center for Naval Analyses had studied the damage done to returning bombers and found bullet holes clustering around the wings, nose, and tail. Put more armor where the bullets tend to hit, they reasoned, and more of our boys and bombers would make it home.

Wald quickly saw the flaw in this logic. Can you? Take a moment to think about it. It's not immediately intuitive, and had it not been for Wald, the navy would have lost endless months, dollars, and lives walking down an obvious and seemingly fruitful path.

Wald stopped the navy in its tracks with one simple question, "What about the bombers that *aren't* returning home?" Perhaps the planes that were being hit in the nose, tail, and wings were the ones that did just fine, coming back to base to share their data. The navy officers were mistakenly assuming that the planes making it home were a random sample of all planes and that bullets just naturally clustered in these locations. It took someone who did not consider himself an expert on planes to offer an obvious, to him, and very different perspective.

The extra armor, Wald reasoned, belonged everywhere else—around the cockpit, for example. Wald's solution carried the day, saved untold lives, and gave the Allies a critical advantage in the skies.

Wald had a finely honed mathematical mind and absolutely no military or aviation experience. So was he an expert or a beginner? The navy had the good sense to use him as an *explorer*, applying his expertise well outside his domain. He was willing to step back from his day-to-day comfortable work to step into the unknown and in doing so made an enormous breakthrough.

If exploring outside our realms of expertise is such a powerful tool for breaking our patterns of thinking, I wondered why it doesn't come more naturally. Why do so many of us stay comfortably in our own domains, inadvertently becoming more fixed and rigid? Why don't more veterans of their fields break up their thinking patterns and win Nobel Prizes? Why is Dane's inverted *U* the rule, not the exception? The culprits, I would find, are two drives we humans have trouble resisting: ego attachment and urgency. Learning to master them, as we'll see next, can open the space to explore much more broadly and get out of the kind of safe thinking that keeps us stuck.

CHAPTER 6

Ego and Urgency

How to tame the urges that keep us from exploring

t's 2007, and Vineet Nayar has just been appointed CEO of HCL Technologies, a global IT services company based in India. His first public appearance is about to get under way. Nayar steps onto the stage as a crowd of 4,000 employees murmurs speculation about what the new boss is going to say. They're about to be shocked, and not by his words.

Nervous anticipation fills the room because Nayar is taking over in uncertain times. The firm has recently grown rapidly to 55,000 employees, and major challenges are on the horizon. HCL is going through the growing pains of transitioning from cut-rate outsource IT provider to aspiring global player, and that will mean having to compete with giants like IBM for some of the world's most demanding customers. Few feel that the company is ready. While revenues are still growing, competitor revenues are growing much faster. Nayar will later liken the situation to standing on the ledge of a burning building with only two choices: pray or leap into the unknown.

Nayar faces the room and smiles. Suddenly, a popular Bollywood tune blasts through the auditorium. The boss begins bopping his head and awkwardly wiggling his portly, middle-aged body. He is dancing!

He descends the stage and boogies his way down the aisle. The employees, nervously at first, begin clapping their hands over their heads. Now they're cheering as he pulls people out into the aisle to dance with him. He shimmies all around the room, employees crushing in behind him, and when he returns to the stage, sweaty and out of breath, the crowd erupts in a cheer.

After performing another number on stage to more raucous approval, Nayar composes himself. He begins to lay out his vision for totally upending the company's management structure, giving more autonomy to frontline employees. He says that he has laid out the bones of the plan but still wants his employees to speak up and challenge it—that their input is vital.

He recalled later, "Those words sounded very different coming from a sweaty man who had just proved in public that he couldn't dance than they would have coming from the emperor at the podium." His goofy ploy worked. An animated, two-hour discussion followed.

Nayar wasn't dancing only for the employees that day; he was also playing a psychological trick on himself. The company's board had given him carte blanche to drive change however he saw fit. But he feared thinking he knew exactly what to do. He wanted to find a way to make sure he listened, genuinely and with a flexible mind, to any and all ideas shared. By humbling himself with his wacky dancing, he primed his psyche to be receptive. After dancing, he felt he had less of an expert's image to defend, having already showed how imperfect he was.

Nayar would repeat his dance routine twenty-five times that year at HCL meetings around the world. Employees from every corner and all levels of the company offered a wealth of insights about how to drive the transformation. Three years later, revenue had tripled. HCL was outcompeting market leaders for major contracts, and the company was a $6 billion powerhouse. Looking back on the transition, Nayar credits the success of the transformation he led to the mind-set he inspired, in his company and in himself, with his humbling dance.

Feeling So Smart We Become Stupid

It feels good to be an expert. It's a mark of accomplishment, intelligence, and hard work. It brings us esteem and makes us feel needed. And that, just like overactive pattern recognition, can lead us, unwittingly, down the path to entrenchment. As we come to identify with what we think we know, our identities and our egos can become attached to the unique knowledge networks we've constructed, leading us to want to defend our expertise from any challenges, whether from new information that runs contrary to our accumulated knowledge or from people questioning our views. The endpoint of this path is closed-mindedness and overconfidence. What's more, the more expertise we develop, and the more we are acknowledged to be expert in a subject, the stronger these effects become.

Remember the miserable performance of Philip Tetlock's experts? Dig a bit deeper into his data, and you'll find that not all experts performed at equal levels. "Super experts," those frequently quoted by the press, highly paid for their opinions, and well known to the public, stood apart. Their predictions about the future were even more miserable, dramatically so.

"There's something about public speaking and having a prominent role in the media that brings out our worst side," Tetlock told me as we discussed his findings. "You don't want to disappoint people so you rush to answers." The lauded expert comes to believe that he sees the world more clearly than others and has little to gain from listening and considering contradictory evidence. Hearing this, I immediately flashed back to my own times on stage speaking about my storytelling theories, confidently batting away questions that ran counter to my way of seeing the world. Tetlock warns that ego-enhancing factors fuel overconfidence, increasing our rate of error and decreasing our ability to learn from those mistakes, or even to notice when we've made them.

How quickly can you come to identify with your own sense of expertise and commit errors because of it? Does it take a spot on CNN or an admiring profile in the *Wall Street Journal*? Or can it happen at any level of accomplishment. For an answer, try this:

First, on a scale of one to seven, how knowledgeable would you say you are about the field of personal finance?

Next, rate your understanding of the following terms, again on a scale of one to seven:

Tax bracket
Fixed-rate mortgage
Home equity

Prerated stocks
Whole life insurance
Roth IRA
Annualized credit
Interest rate
Inflation
Private equity fund
Vesting
Retirement
Fixed-rate deduction
Revolving credit

In 2015, researchers from Cornell and Tulane universities administered this test to one hundred participants, who took it from home on their computers. The test takers didn't know that three of these terms (annualized credit, fixed-rate deduction, and prerated stocks) are completely made up. Nobody could possibly be familiar with them. But many of the participants claimed that they were quite knowledgeable about them, and those who rated themselves highest on the scale of financial expertise were by far the most likely to make this claim.

Keep in mind that participants weren't lying to impress the test administrators; they took the test in the privacy of their homes. They were deluding themselves to protect their self-perceptions of expertise. Additional experiments with such tests about biology, literature, philosophy, and geography produced comparable results.

The problem of overconfidence and closed-mindedness in areas we believe we have expertise is all the more troubling because we so generally tend to credit ourselves with having more expertise than we do. Many studies have documented this phenomenon, often referred to as the "better-than-average effect." For example, 93 percent of US drivers rate themselves as above average behind the wheel. Even drivers currently laid up in the hospital for accidents they themselves had caused were similarly found to overestimate their abilities! Eighty-seven percent of Stanford MBA students rate themselves as more capable than most of their peers. In one British study, prisoners scored themselves as significantly more trustworthy, moral, and honest than the general population.

Perhaps there's little danger in thinking we know quite a bit about "prerated stocks" when in fact they don't exist. But what about believing we know more about the market for our products or about our customers than we really do?

What might the better-than-average effect do to the judgment of business executives evaluating their offering against competitors'? Or to that of investment professionals who have in fact had better-than-average results for a few years in a row? Time and again, an ego investment in one's own ability and expertise leads to disastrous outcomes of overconfidence.

"We are hitting on all 99 cylinders," Jimmy Cayne told a *New York Times* reporter in 2003. "So you have to ask yourself, What can we do better? And I just can't decide what that might be." Five years later, Cayne would lose 95 percent of his billion-dollar net worth and be named by *Time* magazine as one of the twenty-five people to blame for the 2008 financial crisis. Cayne was the CEO of Bear Stearns when he made these comments and when it collapsed.

Remember Nokia? On the day that Apple introduced its iPhone, the Finnish giant had an almost inconceivable 47 percent of market share for mobile phones. Nokia engineers laughed the iPhone off because they thought their batteries were much better, just as they'd turned their noses up at flip phones because they claimed you couldn't open them with one hand. When Stephen Elon took over as CEO of Nokia in 2010, he found a company in shambles. His first message to his team: lose the arrogance. "There's a number of examples over the last six, seven years, where Nokia heard trends but decided to ignore those trends because it felt that it somehow knew better," he observed. "And that hurt the company badly for many years." Elon's insight came too late to save the erstwhile market leader from a fire sale to Microsoft.

It's not easy to overcome the better-than-average effect, especially when one's authority rests on being, well, better than average. Aren't we expected as leaders to have at least some superior powers? When Nayar stepped out and did his awful but memorable dance, he had the intended effect on his audience of one, his ego. But what about his audience of thousands, his employees? In times of uncertainty, don't those who follow us want us to lead with a firm, confident, and, yes, maybe infallible hand? Not as much as we might think. Ample evidence indicates that displaying curiosity and openness is more valued in leaders than providing important answers. Numerous studies have recently shown that self-aggrandizing CEOs tend to make riskier investments, pay higher premiums for acquisitions, and create inconsistent organizational performance. They have worse relationships with their managers.

This data may explain a rising appreciation for humble leaders who act like explorers rather than experts. Instead of making their employees feel uncertain and unguided, according to a 2013 study from the University of Washington and the State University of New York, Buffalo, humble leaders were far more likely to have engaged, satisfied, and loyal employees. This appreciation seems to hold up at the highest levels of achievement. When the *Harvard Business Review* asked prominent management authors to list their gurus, Peter Drucker appeared most often. Second was Stanford's Jim March. March has spent decades researching and publishing prominent papers in behavioral economics, organizational psychology, and statistics. His explorations take him into the fields of literature, film, and poetry. Though the top managers in the world constantly seek his advice, here's how he characterizes the answers he's willing to provide:

> I still occasionally do something I humorously call "consulting" but probably is better seen as getting someone to buy lunch for me. If someone calls me up and says a manager would like to talk to me, I'm inclined to respond that I almost certainly don't have anything useful to say. . . . I think that it would ordinarily be difficult to discover any practical use for such conversations, but I may occasionally have a way of looking at things that is sufficiently different to help a manager in some marginal way. Usually, managers are sensible enough not to ask me to lunch, and I end up paying for most of my lunches myself.

Despite being one of the world's most respected experts across numerous fields, March resists taking on this title. Instead he emphasizes his identity as a committed and avid explorer. What may sound like false modesty is actually key to indicating humility and keeping his ego in check. This allows him to openly ask questions, gain knowledge in new fields, and constantly expand his expertise.

Mastering the Need for Speed

On March 29, 2005, Elaine Bromiley, a healthy mother of two young children, checked into a hospital near her home in Buckinghamshire, England. For years, Bromiley had been bothered by a sinus issue that occasionally caused her face to swell. Her doctor had told her that a routine operation could solve this problem.

Shortly after the anesthetic consultant had put Bromiley under, he determined that her airway had collapsed, and he began trying to put a breathing tube down her throat. After several tries, he issued a call for help, to which an ear, nose, and throat surgeon and a senior anesthetist responded. They too struggled to intubate Bromiley, who had begun to show serious signs of distress.

A well-established protocol in medicine outlines what to do in the event that a patient stops breathing during surgery. As one handbook states, "Do not waste time trying to intubate when the priority is oxygenation." An immediate tracheotomy should be performed.

Yet for twenty more minutes the doctors working on Bromiley continued trying desperately to get the tube in place. The nurses in the room later reported that they wanted to tell the doctors to move on to the tracheotomy, but they were afraid of speaking out of line. The doctors, after all, were the experts. As Bromiley's face turned blue, her hands shot up to her face, and her blood pressure levels swung wildly, one nurse did bring a tracheotomy set to the doctors. They ignored her. Another called the intensive care unit and asked for a bed to be prepared. The doctors told her she was overreacting.

After twenty-five minutes they finally got the tube down Bromiley's throat. But twenty-five minutes without oxygen is an eternity to the human brain. Elaine Bromiley went into a coma. A week later, she was taken off life support. Her healthy heart continued to beat for another week, before she died on April 11.

Bromiley's doctors had latched onto a flawed solution and then got stuck in the effort to make it work despite training that called for them to perform a tracheotomy, despite the nurse's attempt to get them to change course, and despite the clear signs that Bromiley's distress was increasing.

What happened during those harrowing twenty-five minutes, in which the doctors tried in vain to intubate their struggling patient and failed to take an obvious alternative action that would have saved her life, was not the result of inexperience or even necessarily of incompetence. It was a classic case of the expert's rush to judgment when faced with an urgent need to act. Two anesthetists and a surgeon had committed quickly to a reasonable, but ultimately deadly, course of action, and once they did, they were unable to change direction.

We can't expect doctors to be perfect, and errors are inevitable. But as Ian Leslie, who reported Bromiley's story for the *New Statesman*, notes, hospitals are chronically dangerous places. As many as 34,000 deaths per year occur in the United Kingdom due to patient-safety accidents. In the United States, errors are thought to be the third most common cause of death after cancer and heart disease. Globally, you have a one-in-ten chance of leaving a hospital in worse shape than you entered it.

What do people expect from experts when they bring them difficult challenges in urgent situations? Slowly evolving, ambiguous responses? Of course not. Experts are expected to present rapid, firm opinions in the face of uncertainty. But rapidly formed opinions are often flawed, and once formulated, they can be hard to shake. In fact, they can literally distort the way we see reality.

Imagine we make a wager. I will show you a partially blurred image, and you have to guess what it is. You know that about half the people who have seen this blurred image before you have identified it correctly. So it's a fair bet. But now I add a wrinkle. You can choose between two ways of seeing the image. In the first option, we'll start with the partially blurred image, and it will slowly dissolve into extreme blurriness. Then you'll guess. Or you can choose the opposite. We'll begin at extreme blur and slowly proceed to the partially blurred state. Which would you choose? And do you think it matters?

The results of this experiment, run in a laboratory setting with a large number of participants, were startling. Those shown the partially blurred image dissolving into illegibility continued to get it right 50 percent of the time. But those who started in a state of complete ambiguity and moved to resolution got it right only 25 percent of the time! Why? They couldn't resist making early guesses. And once they did, they refused, despite straightforward visual evidence that they were wrong, to change their minds.

Researchers Arie Kruglanski and Donna Webster call this kind of trap "seizing and freezing." They attribute it to what's known as a need for closure, which they have studied extensively. People who display a high need for closure tend to value firm answers to questions and show discomfort when in a state of ambiguity for more than a short period. Facing an unfamiliar challenge, people with high need for closure tend to "seize" on an early solution and then "freeze," meaning they will tend to stick with that solution to the bitter end, focusing on evidence that it's working and dismissing evidence that it's not. Kruglanski and Webster have found that the need to appear highly competent, common, for example, to surgeons, tends to increase the intensity of this trait.

Seizing and freezing provides a sense of stability in high-pressure and quickly developing situations. It makes leaders appear strong and decisive. It also consistently leads to low levels of creativity, poor information processing, and at times disastrous decisions, like those of Elaine Bromiley's doctors.

It makes sense, of course, that the doctors seized on something quickly so they could take action. Their patient needed oxygen, and there wasn't time to consider dozens of possibilities. The question, however, is why they froze upon it. Knowing that they hadn't carefully considered multiple options, wouldn't they be more likely to admit when the chosen course was wrong? Ironically, no. Kruglanski and Webster have shown that the more quickly we take a position on something, the more confident we are in that position. It runs counter to the intuitive notion that the longer you've researched and considered possibilities, the more confident you become. Instead, it's as if our brains believe that because we haven't entertained alternate views, those alternatives simply don't exist, or they're obviously not worthy of consideration. Thus our hastily chosen view stands alone as the right one.

When time is tight and the stakes are high, committing to exploration over expert judgment is extremely difficult. Under duress, we feel we have no choice but to narrow the field of possibility, act decisively, and fall back into the expert mind-set in order to act quickly. Seize and freeze is likely to follow. While we can't avoid finding ourselves in high-pressure situations, we can prepare for them ahead of time, committing to processes designed to work rapidly but also rationally under pressure. After Elaine Bromiley lost her life to a seize-and-freeze error, her husband, Martin, fought to bring such practices into the culture of hospitals.

Martin Bromiley is a veteran airline pilot, and as he heard the blow-by-blow accounts of his wife's failed intubation, sparks of recognition ignited in his mind. For decades, overconfident and autocratic airline pilots had been making very similar mistakes to those of Elaine's surgeons, at a cost of thousands of lives. Bromiley recalls a terrifying but not unusual case in point. On January 8, 1989, British Midland Flight 92 left London for Belfast. Shortly after takeoff, the pilot discovered that one of the engines was on fire. He followed standard operating procedure by shutting down the engine. Everything should have been fine, except that he accidentally shut down the functioning engine, leaving the airplane with no propulsion. When he announced over the PA that there was a problem with the right engine, the entire cabin crew and the passengers could plainly see that in fact the left engine was on fire. They could see what the pilot could not from the cockpit, but nobody, not one person, dared to speak up. Moments later, the plane crashed into an embankment of the M1 motorway. Forty-seven people on board died; seventy-four were seriously injured.

By the 1990s, the airline industry was determined to root out, once and for all, the senseless, consistent mistakes caused by expert rushes to judgment. Fortunately, a solution, under development since the 1970s, was now ready to scale industry-wide. Crew resource management (CRM) set up protocols to undermine the captain's aura of infallibility: giving permission, even responsibility, to anyone who sees a problem to speak up, insisting that pilots be called by their first names, creating expectations for subordinates to make direct and clear suggestions rather than politely suggesting new possibilities. CRM recognizes that by dint of personality, situation, and position, airline pilots have extremely high need for closure. Its systems and culture resist that need until a decision is properly considered and planned.

It may seem that in times of stress and need for decisive action that we should look to the most exalted expert in the room and follow his or her command. That notion seems obvious because it is baked into basic ideas about leadership and hierarchy. Yet, perhaps the highest-stakes industry in the world has discarded it as flawed thinking.

"It's the people at the edge of the room, standing back from the situation, who can often see it best," Bromiley says.

Remember how the nurses were afraid to insist to Elaine Bromiley's doctor that she be given a tracheotomy? That wouldn't happen on an airplane today, and Martin is now determined to make sure it doesn't happen in operating rooms. Like Abraham Wald, who brought a powerful outsider's view to an industry, Bromiley has been quietly revolutionizing UK hospital practice through his Clinical Human Factors Group.

"I'm not an expert on medical practice. I'm just a guy who flies planes," he says. Despite his modesty, he's become one of the world's leading medical reformers.

Martin Bromiley's story teaches us that an effective expert under pressure will slow down as a crisis emerges and listen to opposing or unusual points of view. This takes humility, openness, and calm. If we are in a position of leadership, we must eventually choose one course of action and follow it. That's a given. But if our instinct is to use only a fraction of our given time to choose a course, leaving as much time as possible to execute, we are likely to fall into the seize-and-freeze trap.

Monty Python's John Cleese, whose life-and-death crises have been particularly bloody though fictional, says that opening more time up front, even when under deadline, is also the key to breakthrough creativity. In fact, he says it is key to his comic success:

I was always intrigued that one of my Monty Python colleagues who seemed to be more talented than I was never produced scripts as original as mine. And I watched for some time and then I began to see why. If he was faced with a problem, and fairly soon saw a solution, he was inclined to take it. Even though (I think) he knew the solution was not very original. Whereas if I was in the same situation, although I was sorely tempted to take the easy way out, and finish by 5 o'clock, I just couldn't. I'd sit there with the problem for another hour-and-a-quarter, and by sticking at it would, in the end, almost always come up with something more original. It was that simple. My work was more creative than his simply because I was prepared to stick with the problem longer.

Urgency is a primary driver of a need for closure. And Cleese certainly faced important deadlines in writing his scripts, so he indeed had objective need for closure in his life. Instead of focusing on the general urgency of getting his work done, however, as so many of us do on a deadline, he created a bargain with himself. He would do all the selection and finalization of ideas at the latest possible hour, leaving as much time for exploration up front as possible. What he sacrificed in refinement, he more than made up for in breakthrough originality.

Practicing this sort of decision delay isn't easy. One reason is the common expert practice of creating an early provisional position. One of the easiest ways for the brain to start resolving a highly complex and ambiguous situation is to create a provisional, or tentative, position. We tell ourselves we're only using this position as a stand-in and that we will allow data and ongoing evidence to sway us. Numerous studies have shown that once formulated, a provisional position is enormously difficult to dislodge, even if we have no particular conscious motivation to hold on to it. As explorers rather than experts, our challenge is, like Cleese, to spend just a bit more time in open-minded consideration. Even in an operating room, decisions are rarely as urgent as they seem, and a few more moments of consideration can make all the difference.

LEARNING: KEY TAKEAWAYS

Spend time doing things that make you a beginner again

Engaging in just about anything that is both challenging and unfamiliar creates more cognitive flexibility. Being a rank beginner breaks down overactive pattern recognition, giving you a boost of creativity, even when you return to your area of expertise.

People who live abroad become significantly more creative. Even if you can't leave the country, how can you regularly spend time outside your area of expertise?

Don't bother trying to look like an expert

As Philip Tetlock discovered, the more we project an air of expertise, the more often we're wrong and the slower we are to learn. And though we may fear nobody will follow us if we admit to fallibility, research indicates that people prefer humble leaders.

Vineet Nayar put his ego in check by dancing awfully in front of thousands. What can you do to remind yourself and those you lead that you're aiming to be an explorer, not an expert?

Put off important decisions as long as possible

The more urgent the situation, the more likely we are to "seize" on an obvious solution and then "freeze" on it, blinding ourselves to evidence we're on the wrong track. As the airline industry learned, before urgency cranks up, we need to put practices and commitments in place that force us to slow down, listen to more opinions, and consider broader options.

John Cleese maximized his consideration time by never committing to a course until he absolutely had to. Then, once he had committed, he acted decisively. How can you expand your consideration time, even by 10 percent? The results can be transformative.

PART 4

FLEXIBILITY

CHAPTER 7

The Power and Perils of Thinking with Your Gut

*Why we need intuition and how it
often leads us astray*

" **W**hen they first arrived, many people were hiding," Wilfreda Agul Oketch recalls of the day strangers came to her village in rural Kenya looking for women willing to accept cash, no questions asked. "The people thought they were Illuminati who would drain our blood. Who gives unconditional money?" Oketch had her own fears of the newcomers, but she says, speaking to me through a translator, that her problems were dire enough to lead her to step forward. "My house was made of iron sheets. I had no bed. No chair."

A few days later, Oketch remembers her son running to her. "'Why are you crying that you have no money?' he asked me. 'Look, it says right here on your phone the money has come through!'" Oketch had received 10,000 Kenyan shillings, about $100. With this first transfer, she says, she bought a metal door and a solar lamp so she would no longer have to buy paraffin to light her home. Next, she plastered her walls so she could stop smearing dung on them regularly to keep the rain out. When I asked her how long it might have taken to save enough money for these improvements on her own, she paused for some time. "Never," she replied.

Weeks passed, and nobody came for Oketch's blood or asked her for anything for that matter. Oketch had enrolled in a radically unusual aid program run by an organization called GiveDirectly. Their model: give money to the poorest, no questions asked. Ian Bassin, who manages donor relations for GiveDirectly, admits the approach sounds irresponsible, if not nefarious, as some of its recipients viewed it at first. "I mean, we are asking people to do something that I think most people are instinctively psychologically resistant to," he says.

Which of these two statements do you agree with?

Give a man a fish, feed him for a day. Teach a man to fish, feed him for a lifetime.
or
The best way to help a man in need is to just give him money.

Nearly everyone chooses the first one, and that's true both for those who donate a few dollars to help hungry kids and for those who have doled out billions in international aid and conducted extensive analysis of charitable giving. The idea that poor people lack not just money but also knowledge of the best way to spend it or the responsibility to spend it in constructive ways has been a truism. This is why most charities either spend money for people or create programs to educate them about better ways to live.

Michael Faye, Paul Niehaus, and their team at GiveDirectly began to think it might be a mistake to allow the prevailing approach to international aid to stand untested. Faye was an economics graduate student at Harvard when he and a few friends wondered if poor people actually knew better than anyone else what they needed. Indeed, they had seen that countries like Brazil and Mexico had replaced some forms of public assistance with direct cash payments and seen surprisingly good results. So they decided to create a small giving circle designed to offer cash awards of $1,000 each to the poorest people in Kenya. Due to the widespread adoption of mobile phones in the country, the friends found they'd be able send cash directly to recipients' devices, without relying on the traditional chain of middlemen. They'd test the results rigorously. Aside from that, there was nothing more to the program. No advice to recipients. Nothing out of bounds to spend the money on. No teaching anyone to fish.

The preliminary results were extremely encouraging. Grantees were making smart choices in spending the money, getting long-deferred medical care, starting businesses, and investing in sturdier roofs (a high-return, long-term investment). There was no increase in alcohol consumption or gambling, as conventional wisdom predicted. More than 90 percent of the money they put into the program was going directly to recipients.

When Margaret Adoyo Rachuonyo, another recipient I spoke to, received her transfer from GiveDirectly, she knew exactly what to do with it. "I was the laughing stock of the village because I couldn't afford to send my orphaned granddaughter to high school. With the money, I bought books, a uniform, and sent her to school."

These encouraging stories were consistent with the positive results coming in from evaluations from external academics. At that point, Faye says, he felt the model was ready to scale. "We shared the idea around, and lots of people thought we were nuts," he told me. "I remember one HBS professor suggesting we start a microfinance organization instead. Google.org said, 'You're smoking crack but show us the evidence.'"

They did, and not long afterward, Google granted them $2 million. A couple years later, GiveDirectly received $25 million more from the foundation of Dustin Moskovitz, a cofounder of Facebook, and his wife, Cari Tuna. A few years after that, the organization had raised more than $130 million for recipients, to be given away, no questions asked. Today, GiveDirectly is consistently rated one of the most effective charities in the world.

Why has the old "teach a man to fish" adage held such sway? Not because of extensive evidence but because it seems so right. I'll bet it still does to you, even after reading about GiveDirectly. That's because we've heard that we should teach a man to fish, in one form or another, so many times that it's become intuitive. We don't have to think about whether it's right. We just know, at a gut level, that it is.

Now consider Faye's counterargument. People in the richer, developed world observe that many of the poor around them are mentally ill, traumatized, and on the outskirts of society. Poverty in the developed world is a complex social phenomenon, and it's common to have very particular notions and biases about those in its clutches. But in many developing countries, profound poverty is just the result of being born there. These people are not societal outcasts and are quite capable of participating in the mainstream. Does this insight begin to change your intuition? It changed that of Faye and his colleagues, and due to their impressive results, it's now changing the intuition of the entire development field.

Brilliant Ideas That Look Insane to (Almost) Everyone

Breakthroughs often come from pursuing ideas that seem counterintuitive to most people and therefore crackpot. They may even, at first, seem counterintuitive to those who pursue them, but some ignored information leads them to suspect that perhaps the prevailing wisdom is wrong and convinces them to proceed, often in the face of rejection or even ridicule. Not long ago, anyone could have told you that people would never willingly hop into a stranger's car, sleep in the apartment of someone they've never met, or upload their most important and sensitive files to some abstract realm called the cloud. Like giving away money no questions asked, such business models flew in the face of a basic shared intuition about what's possible. Why not let people sell their leftover food while you're at it? (Indeed, similar ideas have been tried with considerably less success.)

These businesses were wildly counterintuitive until a few people believed in them enough to build them. Before long they became the most intuitive way to hail a cab, rent a room, or store your data. In fact, it's now hard to imagine life without them.

By their very nature, counterintuitive ideas lead the way to possibilities few others are interested in considering, and this is a key reason that, according to esteemed creativity researcher Robert Sternberg, they can be such rich sources of creative breakthrough. Sternberg likens creative people to good investors in that they are bold enough to spend time and often money on ideas that "are viewed as novel and perhaps slightly ridiculous." Creative individuals, he says, are often adept at spotting chances "to buy low and sell high in the world of ideas." They repeatedly invest in these low-value ideas and then reap the rewards when they gain acceptance.

Of course, plenty of counterintuitive ideas are, in fact, off base. Things that seem wrong often seem wrong for a reason. So when we're considering pursuing a counterintuitive idea, how can we determine whether or not to proceed? When beating an entirely new path, there's rarely enough data available to make a rock solid analytic case. Moving forward takes courage and a high degree of resolve to follow the counterintuitive route.

Where does that courage and resolve come from? Because analysis alone can't prove the unusual idea is right, proceeding demands a heavy dose of intuition. Thus, somewhat ironically, counterintuitive breakthroughs often come not when we ignore our own intuition but when we invest in it at just the right time.

Perhaps this is why leaders at the top levels of complex businesses so often point to their intuition as their greatest asset. GE's Jack Welch said that good decisions come "straight from the gut." Ralph Larsen, former CEO of Johnson & Johnson, famously claimed that level of intuition separates mid-level from senior management. And even as the world has become more data rich, intuition, surprisingly, is still an executive's most favored tool. A 2014 survey of more than 1,000 executives found that business leaders relied most often on intuition, beating out data and the advice of others.

So, should we run headlong into feeling our way to ideas others find bizarre? Not so fast. Powerful as it may be, intuition can be fickle and unreliable. Some of the messages that we take to be intuition—or gut feelings—are not the authentic article. They can be replete with biases, internalized conventional wisdom, and false pattern recognition.

In the next three chapters, we'll explore the landscape of intuition with the goal of learning how to generate risky but ultimately intelligent buy-low-sell-high ideas that seem counterintuitive to most. First, we'll determine where intuition, an often mysterious sense of knowing, arises from and why we need it to navigate uncertainty. While an indispensable guide, intuition can be deceiving. So we'll look at how to pick apart good intuition from bias and faulty assumptions. For those willing to interrogate their own gut instincts, science provides plenty of tools for sharpening and honing intuitive skills. Finally, with a deeper sense of mastery over our own intuitive processes, we'll look at how to develop ideas that seem off base to most but in fact hold enormous creative potential.

Our Hidden Genius

Everyone experiences intuition daily. We assess a complex situation, and then, in a flash, a feeling of knowing pervades us. We don't follow logic or a set of clues, then reason our way to a point of view. Instead, we get an emotional sense, often accompanied by bodily sensations, that ultimately coalesces into a conscious thought. Hence, we often say we feel intuition in our gut.

So where do these feelings of knowing come from?

What we commonly call "intuition" actually refers to a couple of very different mental processes that we experience in very similar ways. The first we might simply call subconscious processing, in which our brain is logically analyzing information in the background of our conscious attention, and when it arrives at a sense of coherence, an intuition bursts forth. This type of intuition uses similar neural pathways in the brain as those used for conscious thinking, so its conclusions, while hard to explain and justify, can be as "smart" as those derived by our conscious mind. In fact, this type of intuition has some advantages over conscious thinking. Our underground reasoning has access to far more information than we can otherwise consider. Researchers liken our attention to an iceberg, with conscious thought equating to the portion above the surface. We can observe it and are aware of its existence. Our subconscious attention, on the other hand, is below the surface, made of similar stuff though unobservable and covering far more territory. This understanding of subconscious processing goes a long way to demystifying intuition from some form of magic to a much more familiar way of thinking, just happening where we can't see it. Herbert Simon, one of the most oft-cited psychologists of the twentieth century, went so far as to say that intuition is "simply analysis frozen into habit." He explains, "All the time, we are reaching conclusions on the basis of things that go on in our perceptual system, where we're aware of the result of the perception but we're not aware of the steps."

Here's one reason subconscious processing seems so exotic to our logical minds: its sense of knowing travels from underwater to the surface not by way of our recently evolved verbal or rational neural pathways but through much older systems that carry sensation and feelings. This partially explains why the signals of intuition are, at first, physical and emotional, and this is why we get a "gut feel" without being able to explain why.

The second source of intuition relies on what Daniel Kahneman and Amos Tversky have famously referred to as "heuristics," mental shortcuts that we use to quickly and efficiently make sense of a complex world. In other words, snap judgments. Heuristics are hard-coded deeply in our psychological makeup, often regardless of experiences we've had. We don't learn these shortcuts so much as we're born with them. For example, we intuitively "know" that things that happen in close succession and close proximity are probably related through cause and effect (even when they're not). Another heuristic tells us that if we want to know how trustworthy someone is likely to be, we can simply compare their characteristics to other trustworthy people we've known.

Heuristics are not the same as the first intuitive process of analysis happening beneath the surface; the two processes tend to employ different regions of the brain. Kahneman and others call the mental processes heuristics use "System 1," while analysis works off an entirely different system, "System 2."

Different as these phenomena are, these two types of intuition feel much the same. Like subconscious processing, heuristic thinking tends to transmit its findings through the body and through feelings. The instantaneousness of both processes also makes them feel quite similar. Subconscious processing often takes considerable time, but because we're not aware that our brains are working in the background, the resulting intuition may feel like it happens all at once. Heuristic thinking, on the other hand, does happen at lightning speed. That's why Kahneman calls it "thinking fast."

Of course, these two types of intuition are not the only ones that serious scholars, philosophers, psychologists, and mystics have identified. Across cultures, people have spoken of intuitive senses of knowing that come from tapping into a collective source of wisdom, from hallucinogenic drug experiences, or from deeply felt subjective religious experience. These types of intuition are beyond the scope of this book. For now, we'll limit the definition of intuition to the types science can best observe: subconscious processing and heuristic thinking.

At its best, the power of intuition is astonishing. Take a few cases in point.

A Formula One driver approaches a hairpin bend, one that he's practiced maneuvering through at high speed thousands of times. But this time he gets a sudden urge to brake hard, and he does, just in time to avoid an unseen pileup of cars on the track ahead. He has no idea why he chose to brake. He does know the decision probably saved his life. Only after watching a video of the event with a group of forensic psychologists does he realize what clue his subconscious brain picked up on. The video reveals that the crowd wasn't watching him but was staring rigidly farther down the track, indicating something ahead was very wrong.

Wolfgang Mozart writes a letter to a friend explaining the process by which he creates symphonies. "Whence and how they come I know not," he explains. "Nor do I hear in my imagination the parts successively, but I hear them, as it were, all at once. For this reason, the committing to paper is done quickly enough, for everything is, as I've said before, already finished. And it rarely differs on paper from what it is in my imagination." Mozart describes these presentations of his subconscious as accompanied by a sense of utter delight. He can enjoy them almost as if someone else had written them. That is how far they originate from his conscious mind.

Participants in a study at Tel Aviv University receive a seemingly impossible mathematical challenge. They are asked to choose which group of numbers, those on the left or the right, have a higher average. Two to four pairs of numbers are flashed on the screen, changing every two seconds. There is hardly enough time to even see all the numbers, let alone add them up, do the division, and then compare their averages. When shown six pairs, participants choose the correct answer 65 percent of the time—far better than chance. Shown twenty-four pairs, a truly mind-numbing amount, they "guess" right—and it does feel like guessing—90 percent of the time. By completely overwhelming their conscious brains, researchers unlock a genius that nearly all the participants possess.

In accord with these three examples of intuition in action, researchers have identified three circumstances in which relying on our intuition is particularly advised. The first is when time is of the essence. The Formula One driver doesn't have the luxury of weighing all his options. It's just brake or don't. Relying on his intuition saves his life. The second circumstance is when a problem is complex and without concrete definition. Writing a masterpiece symphony is just such a problem. Though guidelines and precedents about what makes for a great work can assist, they cannot account for creative originality. In the vacuum where established rules and analysis fail, intuition becomes increasingly valuable. And third, intuition is needed when there is too much or too little information. The math study participants, because they were flooded with data, simply had no choice but to rely on their intuitive, likely heuristic, sense of the right answer. The more they were forced to do so, the more accurate their calculations became.

Intuition gives us access to our own otherwise inaccessible genius, and we need that in a world awash with conventional wisdom that is at once confidently certain and also outdated or premised on faulty assumptions. To spot patterns that others have missed, to "buy low and sell high" in the world of creative ideas, to persist in the face of rejection and scorn, we need to leverage this critical thinking capacity.

Critical as it may be, however, intuition is certainly not always smarter than (or even as smart as) conscious analytic thought. Just like our conscious minds, our subconscious minds can spot false patterns and lead us to false conclusions. We can internalize adages like "teach a man to fish" after hearing it so often that it pervades our subconscious knowledge systems. And tellingly, the word "heuristic" is often used interchangeably with "bias." Heuristics work in many circumstances, but in others they can lead us badly astray.

The Myth of the Golden Gut

Few people are as renowned for their superior intuitive abilities as Silicon Valley investors. Even in a world that has become complex and ambiguous for everyone, the challenges in this line of work stand apart. Angel investors and venture capitalists must make rapid judgments often with both too much and too little information at their disposal. The problems they invest in solving are often ill defined and unprecedented. They thrive when they see patterns others can't and earn their reputations by spotting ingenious, often counterintuitive, business models that disrupt the world.

The landscape these investors inhabit appears navigable only with strong intuition, and you'll often hear them touting their dependence upon it. But how good is their intuition really? And are they able to tell the difference between reliable intuitions, which can help them spot opportunities others miss, and biased, unfounded intuitions, which will send them following the herd? This may sound like a question with no firm answer, but data is now offering a sobering image of this industry of kingmakers. It's an answer that should give all of us an important clue about how intuition works—and doesn't.

With tens of billions of angel and venture dollars changing hands every year, Wharton's Laura Huang thought it'd be useful to know what was really going on in investors' heads when they choose which companies to put money into. For example, when you've got $50,000 to commit to a company that for now is just a glimmer of an idea but could one day return tens of millions of dollars, how do you even begin to decide which to choose? Do angel investors pick their investments based on the pitch deck they receive, a broader market analysis, personal affinity with the entrepreneur, or perhaps just a gut feel about what might one day be a home run? Huang could have simply asked these investors, but she knows that when it comes to complex decision making, people are notoriously lousy at accurately reporting their own processes. So she and a few collaborators planted themselves for two years inside five angel investment firms and watched, blow by blow, what was actually going on.

Huang's analysis of the data sheds fascinating light on what, until now, has been a process shrouded in mystery and myth. She discovered that early-stage investors consciously grouped their areas of attention into two categories. The first was data—the stuff they gleaned from the financials and strategies presented by the entrepreneur, a broader understanding of market conditions, and any other numbers they could crunch in spreadsheets. Here they were using pure step-by-step analysis. The second area they focused their attention on was their perception of the entrepreneur him- or herself. Did they trust this person? Did he or she look, sound, or otherwise have the bearing of someone who'd brought them success before? Did the investment feel right? This data didn't get processed in spreadsheets. Here, investors unabashedly relied on emotion and intuition.

"That's how I make my decision. . . . I just use my gut feel. . . . You have to go with your gut, and I've always been glad when I did," one investor told Huang's investigators. "You notice right away," reported another investor, "sometimes within five seconds of meeting the entrepreneur, how you feel about them and what your overall sense is for them as a person." Unlike the rigid experts Tetlock studied, these investors weren't consciously applying a mental model. They were listening to their feelings, their bodies. Huang says she's heard investors say, "You know, I invest because I rub my tummy, and that's how I make my investment."

The investors Huang studied were mostly looking for those opportunities in which the data and the gut feel matched up. In an ideal situation, she says,

business viability + feeling about the entrepreneur = decision

But here's the problem with this simple formula: these investors are looking for what they call "home runs," cheap opportunities to invest that nobody else sees. That's how they buy low and sell high. In the obvious cases in which business viability is enormous and the entrepreneur is totally appealing, everyone's trying to invest. It's too late for the home run. To snatch up the hidden opportunities, they need to get a bit counterintuitive in terms of what everyone else sees. They have to be willing to invest when the formula doesn't quite add up, when the data conflicts a bit with the ineffable charisma of the entrepreneur. So which side do they favor when the two don't agree? They lean heavily toward intuition about the person and away from analysis. One investor described this common strategy this way: "I try and spot the diamond in the rough, which is something so ridiculous that it could actually work, because you have the right person willing to take it from ridiculous to completely disruptive." Or, as another put it more bluntly, "I don't care about the financials . . . the business plan . . . as much as I care about the entrepreneur. My most successful deals have come when I trust my gut feelings . . . when I trust only what my gut tells me about the entrepreneur, and filter everything else out."

"Intuition trumped any business data they had," Huang concluded.

Huang shed a lot of light on the use of intuition in early-stage investing, but I also wondered about the bigger money. Once a business gets its angel round and begins to grow, it starts to look for venture funding, which invests millions, not thousands, of dollars. Is intuition still a driving force here? For answers, I sought out Trish Costello. Costello hasn't done the academic analysis that Huang has; instead she draws her perspective from having helped to found the modern field of venture capitalism.

In 1991, Charles Ewing Kauffman, a pharmaceutical executive and billionaire, decided what he wanted to do with his fortune. He would become a philanthropist in a field nobody had ever brought philanthropy to before: entrepreneurship. He tapped Costello to join the foundation's executive team.

"The whole thing was so visionary that the IRS spent several years just trying to figure out if entrepreneurship had a social benefit," Costello says of setting up the nonprofit, which she would lead for fifteen years. "Right away, by law we had to spend $100 million a year. So we were looking to have the biggest impact possible. Up until that point, venture was a cottage industry. It was just East Coast wealthy families. We knew training entrepreneurs would be useful, but training VCs would have an exponential impact on many thousands of entrepreneurs in whom they would invest."

Costello says that Kauffman-trained VCs now invest $45 billion a year. She's seen the industry evolve and mature over the years, but one aspect has remained fairly constant: VCs rely enormously on gut feel to make their investment decisions.

"They'll say you just know it. Your fingers tingle," Costello, who now runs Portfolia, an investment fund focused on bringing more women into the field, says of the common experience of venture investors. "And VCs like to maintain this mystique. Intuition is not something you can teach, and they think that makes them special. There are some rare VCs who have the touch. But for many, it's a pattern recognition that doesn't serve them well."

At this point in the conversation, Costello asked if I'd read the Diana Report. I said I would. And here's where a good deal of the mythology of superior intuition in Silicon Valley comes crashing down.

Between 2011 and 2013, companies with female CEOs received $1.5 billion in venture capital investment, while companies led by men received thirty-four times that amount. Eighty-five percent of companies receiving venture funding had not a single woman on the executive team. The Diana Report, written by researchers at Babson College, has been tracking venture's bias against investing in women since 1999, and the results have been disappointing, to say the least.

Investor intuition rests largely on a gut feeling about the person pitching, and investors' guts tend to think women don't know much about running a successful business. In fact, a 2014 Harvard study found that when men and women pitched the same idea, experienced investors were 60 percent more likely to invest when the idea came from a guy. The industry is engaged in clear pattern recognition, but is it accurate? Does this internal sense of knowing lead, like it did in the case of the Formula One driver or the Tel Aviv number estimators, to effective decision making, even if, in this case, it isn't politically correct?

For investors who think they have a golden gut, the data doesn't look good. Women, it turns out, tend to be more successful, not less, when they lead ventures. A recent study of 22,000 publicly traded companies found that an increase in leadership positions for women from 0 to 30 percent is associated with an increase of 15 percent in a company's profitability. Remember that 85 percent of venture-backed companies are in that 0 percent camp when it comes to women leaders. The Kauffman Foundation recently found that female tech entrepreneurs, on average, generated a 35 percent higher return on investment than their male counterparts. Start-ups with five or more females were found to have a

61 percent success rate compared to a typical 25 to 50 percent rate in the industry. We can stop there, though the damning studies don't.

"For so many years, the thinking was that women need to do certain things to fix themselves," Candida Brush, one of the authors of the Diana Report, explained to me. "But that's not the case anymore. The numbers show it. The industry is broken." These are strong words about an industry that has made billions on visionary investments in recent years. But those home runs, while easy to point to, are rarer than they should be. Since 1997, less cash has made its way back to investors than has been poured into venture funding. For the past decade, VC returns haven't beaten public markets. It seems these intuitive geniuses are, on the whole, providing limited, or even negative, value for investors.

"They're the disruptors of the world, but it's hard for them to see they're being disrupted until it's on them," says Costello of the VC culture she helped to create.

Brush said that while it might seem that pointing to this obvious blind spot in the market would lead to a rush of investors using this data to buy low where nobody else was investing, the VC community has done no more than shrug.

"We got a billion media hits when we released this report," Brush says. "I did so much TV, so much radio. One venture firm called and said they wanted to do something about it. *One.*"

"A very successful VC told me recently that investing in women was a purely PR issue," said Costello with a note of resignation.

So what's happening here? Investors who should behave rationally are relying heavily on gut instinct, which is often cueing them with something other than the subconscious genius that intuition can provide. Instead of moving toward opportunities with women-led businesses, they're herding away from them. When confronted with endless data to prove this reality, they choose to do nothing.

"Investors who use their intuition can spot amazing investments," Huang concluded from her research. But she also told me they can get confused. "You can say you're using gut feel, but you may be using it as a cover to go into biased thinking."

We've seen how powerful intuition can be in helping us recognize patterns in conditions of complexity and when speed of decision making is vital, and that intuition is an indispensable part of creativity. But we've got to be alert about false intuitions that can trap us, leading us to decisions based on biases we would never consciously embrace. Understanding how to watch out for these biases so that we can leverage true intuition while ignoring false messages that keep us stuck in seemingly safe but deeply flawed ways of thinking is our necessary next step.

CHAPTER 8

Harnessing Intuition

*How to recognize faulty intuition
and hone your instincts*

et's put your intuition to the test. Would you say more
words in the English language start with *k* or have a *k* as
their third letter?

An analytic approach to this answer would require a dictionary and
a lot of time. An intuitive approach should give you an answer almost
instantly. When Daniel Kahneman and Amos Tversky asked a lot of
smart people this question, they got a lot of wrong answers. More than
two-thirds of respondents said that *k* appears more often as the first letter than as the third letter in English words. In truth, a typical English
text contains twice the number of words with *k* in the third position.

Fooled by Shortcuts

So why is most people's intuition on this question so wrong? And why
does it matter? Kahneman and Tversky's explanation shook the world's
view of human decision making and led to Kahneman's winning a Nobel
Prize. They demonstrated that what feels like intuition can often just be
faulty heuristic thinking or bias. In this case, test subjects fell victim to
what's known as "availability bias." This thinking flaw causes people to
consistently overweight the importance or likelihood of things that are

easy to recall. It's easier to think of words like "kite," "kitten," and "kick," though there are far more words like "lake," "like," and "dike."

One of Laura Huang's investors describes the availability bias at work when proudly recalling an investment he avoided based on intuition. "[The entrepreneur] was playing in a $65 billion market, and I believed that what he was trying to do could capture a really large chunk of that market." Note, he's describing his analytic system at work. Now watch the intuitive thinking kick in. "But there was something about him that reminded me of why I lost [a large sum of money] on [a prior investment]. He had that same zany glare in his eyes as [the prior entrepreneur], and was using the same 'if . . . then' statements that just took me back to my past nightmare and told me to . . . back away from a $65 billion market. . . . [W]ho does that? It was one of the most painful choices, and I lost a lot of sleep over that one."

This big loss the investor had sustained obviously had a memorable impact on him. So when he saw certain characteristics in this entrepreneur, he felt a strong confidence that he was recognizing a pattern and that he should stay away. Boom, no analysis needed—the decision is made. So what happens when a female entrepreneur steps in front of an intuitive male investor? Remember, he's aware that he's looking for an "it feels right" experience with this entrepreneur, but he's not sure what that means. He just knows it when he sees it. Behind the scenes, his brain searches for easy-to-recall, positive emotional experiences that he can match to this woman. But of course she doesn't, on the surface, look, act, or speak like the previous male entrepreneurs he's invested in. As with those words with *k* in the middle, it's much harder to recall a match for her. The likelihood of her succeeding suddenly seems diminished. Perhaps at this point his rational analytic mind tells him, "You know we really should be giving a second look to women," but his intuitive brain just "knows" this opportunity isn't right. So he passes. But while he thinks his gut is recognizing a pattern, it's overrelying on trivial or limited information.

If availability bias doesn't get the venture investor, the familiarity bias often will. This bias pushes us to prefer investments in the known over the unknown, even when the numbers don't work in our favor. It leads average novice 401(k) investors to put 30 percent of their investable pension money in their own company's stock. It leads German business students to be more optimistic about German stocks than US stocks, and vice versa for American students. It even leads professional money managers to heavily overinvest in regionally based companies on behalf of their clients, and this happens in every region of the country. Nothing about these bias-driven choices is rational; yet this behavior is so widespread that it appears nearly irresistible. How does this help explain an irrational skepticism for women-led businesses? Consider this: Less than one in ten venture capitalists is a woman. Female entrepreneurs usually face a roomful of men whose brains are primed to look for opportunities to invest in people familiar to them.

"Usually people become VCs because they cashed out of a business," Babson College's Candida Brush explains. "They bring people from their old firm to come work with them. It's often just four guys they know really well. They find it very safe to stay in that same lane, go to the same sources for deals."

When a VC faces the unfamiliar, his first impulse is not always to pass on the deal, however. A number of the women I spoke with shared an even more frustrating common experience: "They'll say, let me go home and talk to my wife about it," Trish Costello told me. "Women are coming in with a boatload of data, and they're just taking it down to an N of 1." It's as if the investor subconsciously recognizes that a female entrepreneur feels unfamiliar and jumps to the solution that perhaps his wife will find her easier to understand. "She's not like me, but if she's like my wife, maybe this could work."

After a string of such experiences, Sarah Nadav, founder of a start-up called Civilize, took to Medium to vent her frustration.

Investors, you should know that the only thing that I have in common with your wife is a vagina. . . . You might not realize it, but you compare us to your wives out loud all the time. And we cringe while you do it, and we talk about it with each other, and would like to tell you to STFU every single time but we can't, because we want to get funded so we are nice to you. . . . If you are wondering why you aren't getting pitched by female founders—know this and let it soak in—We talk to each other. We warn each other. If there aren't any women pitching you, it's not a pipeline problem. The problem is literally you.

The story Nadav tells shows how familiarity bias can snowball. Men prefer entrepreneurs like them. They subtly and not so subtly make that known in pitch meetings. Women not only get less funding; they get demoralized or angry. They stop showing up with opportunities, and the image of a woman entrepreneur becomes yet less familiar to these investors.

The work on cognitive biases shows that an investor's reluctance to bet on women founders need not involve the conscious belief that a woman's place is in the home or that having a baby will soon distract her from her work. And heuristic biases are sticky. When shown evidence that contradicts their biased judgment, people don't easily change their minds. In fact, they most often become even more wedded to their views. We see this going on when investors read the Diana Report, learn that they are missing opportunities, and yet still rely on their gut feeling that a woman-run firm just isn't a good bet.

Fooled by Emotion

Cognitive biases are devilish and difficult to overcome. But they aren't alone in skewing our intuition. Because intuition travels to our attention along our emotional highways, it can often get muddled and polluted by feelings that have their own, often unhelpful, agendas.

◇◇◇◇◇◇◇

An Wang carried a grudge with him everywhere, tucked neatly into the jacket pocket of his finely tailored suits. The little paper scorecard tracked his company's progress against that of his enemy, IBM, and he said it kept him focused and hungry.

The slim, bow-tied executive did not come across as an angry man. Those who knew him described Wang as shy and respectful. But, according to biographer Sidney Finkelstein, he harbored an intense anger toward IBM due to a belief that the company had cheated him early in his career. The fierceness of Wang's desire to avenge that wrong is expressed in the edgy combativeness of a memorable ad Wang Laboratories ran in 1985. It features a self-satisfied IBM executive sitting at his desk, gleefully swatting flies, which represent the competition. Then a heavily armed military chopper rises up behind his desk, and a voice ominously warns, "Wang. We're gunning for IBM."

Wang had left China in 1945 and arrived in the United States nearly penniless. By 1947 he had made his way through a master's program at Harvard, and four years later he had invented the magnetic pulse memory core, a donut-shaped piece of metal that would become an important component in early computers. Wang knew his invention would be enormously valuable, and he offered to license his pending patent to IBM. At the time, he admired the company as the gold standard in electronics. But the negotiations went poorly from the outset. In his autobiography, Wang described IBM's tactics as a "no-holds-barred-style of competition." At first, he only found IBM's approach off-putting. As the conversations stretched on, however, the negotiations turned outright hostile. Then, at the worst possible moment, another inventor suddenly filed a lawsuit challenging Wang's claim to the patent. Wang suspected IBM was behind the man's suit, but he couldn't prove anything, and with his negotiating position shot, he had to settle for a $400,000 deal, which was far less than the parties had originally been discussing. Wang eventually won the suit, and not long afterward, he believed his suspicions about IBM's involvement were confirmed. The other inventor died, and Wang asserted without proof that the man's family admitted that IBM had put him up to making the claim. It was then, Wang said, that he vowed he would make IBM pay. And he would succeed, jamming a multi-billion-dollar thorn in the behemoth's side for decades.

Building off his first disappointing deal, Wang turned his attention to the future of calculators (another industry dominated by IBM), which he envisioned would involve electronic rather than mechanical parts. He moved quickly on his insight, building some of the world's most advanced machines throughout the 1960s. His confidence in his judgment was building, and Wang was developing into a classic intuition-driven leader. Soon he made another brilliant call. At the height of his company's success in the calculator market, he suddenly declared that the market would soon be saturated and that it was time to move on.

"Markets change, tastes change, so the companies and the individuals who choose to compete in those markets must change," he wrote. Wang dismissed enormous internal pressure to keep the calculator business going and moved the company into developing some of the world's first word processors. Adding to the pleasure of the success with the new machines was that this move again stepped on the toes of IBM, which generated a large portion of its revenue from typewriters.

By 1983, Wang Laboratories was a juggernaut. It achieved 60 percent growth annually in the early 1980s, and its word-processor business seemed invulnerable. A competitive product had just emerged, however, that would completely disrupt the computing business: the personal computer. And IBM was leading the way. That year, *Time* magazine hailed the newly popular personal computer as the "Machine of the Year." Wang, like a jealous father, lashed out, calling the PC "the stupidest thing I ever heard of."

Despite having everything he needed to jump from word processors to PCs, Wang hesitated to enter the market. He associated the PC with IBM, and investing in PCs might mean the demise of his beloved Wang word processor. He was as confident as ever in his intuition, carried by his strong emotion, but this time he wasn't seeing the right pattern. Wang would begrudgingly enter the PC market, and even then it wasn't too late. Unfortunately, the founder's hatred led to another bold, counterconventional, and wrong decision to make computers that were not IBM compatible, opting instead for a Wang-only system. The Wang PC never caught on, and by 1990 the company was in shambles. Wang died soon after.

An Wang's leap away from the thriving business of calculators and into the emerging field of word processors is a superb example of how following an intuition that strikes others as seriously counterintuitive, and therefore deeply flawed, can lead to creative breakthroughs. But his story also illustrates the danger that we might believe a judgment we're making is a brilliant intuition when it's actually the product of misguided emotion.

Some recent research into how being in tune with our feelings while making a judgment affects our actions demonstrates starkly how our emotions can mislead us. Barnaby Dunn, a researcher at the University of Cambridge, wanted to see if he could capture intuitive decision making right at the moment of its birth. To do so, he set up a study in which participants would try to master a card game that had no obvious strategy for winning. The game wasn't random, however; there were rather difficult-to-ascertain ways to get better at it. Before beginning, Dunn hooked each participant up to instruments that measured their heart rates and sweat production.

Most of the players eventually arrived at a preferred strategy, but they couldn't describe what those strategies were, reporting that they relied on gut instinct or intuition rather than reason. Dunn could see that as the players began to formulate a strategy, their heart rates increased, and they began to sweat from their fingertips. This sent a signal to their brains to follow the strategy. Measuring players' awareness of those physiological changes, Dunn found that some were highly aware, while others were hardly aware at all. The more aware players acted on the signal to pursue their strategy much more quickly. That doesn't mean, however, that their strategies were always helpful.

For some, acting faster meant winning quickly. But for others, listening to their feelings led them quickly to a dead end. This shows that the more attuned we are to our emotions, the more confidently we'll act on intuition. It doesn't mean, however, that our emotions are a flawless guide.

Interrogating Intuition

With so much stacked against us as we try to determine whether we should go with our gut or not, what can we do? If we want to find and invest in counterintuitive breakthroughs, abandoning our intuition altogether hardly seems reasonable, but if it's so often flawed, is letting it guide us ever advisable?

I asked these questions of every intuition researcher who would speak to me. They all gave me slightly different answers, but their advice made essentially the same point.

Robin Hogarth, a leader in the field of intuition research, summed it up elegantly: "Emotions are data that need to be explained." In other words, Hogarth told me, we should treat our intuitive insights like ingenious hypotheses. We shouldn't ignore them. We also shouldn't feel sheepish about openly discussing them with our colleagues. Intuitions should be celebrated. They belong at the front of the line of our attention when making difficult decisions in uncertain environments. But as with hypotheses, we should never trust our intuitions until we've questioned them, pressure-tested them, and patted them down, searching for cognitive and emotional bias.

Easy to say. But I wanted to know how we can make this a part of daily practice. I found the academic texts somewhat vague on the subject, so I began to look for organizations that both relied on and regularly challenged intuition.

◇◇◇◇◇◇◇◇

I wasn't sure what kind of mood I might find Ed Catmull in when I visited his Emeryville, California, office in early 2017. The Oscars were about a month away. For the first time in what felt like forever, Pixar, the company Catmull had cofounded and now led, hadn't earned a best animated feature nomination. The press had begun to question if the studio was losing its creative edge. Sure, *Finding Dory* had grossed more than $1 billion worldwide in 2016, but few thought it deserved mention in the same breath as Disney's *Zootopia* and *Moana*. Disney outcreating Pixar? It would have seemed impossible a decade ago. Sure, Catmull could take much of the credit for Disney's success—he's also president of Walt Disney Animation Studios—but I wondered if he might not be somewhat defensive about the outflanking of Pixar, which he'd run so much longer. Instead he seemed delighted by the turn of events. Things, he said, were going pretty much according to plan. The two studios were pushing each other forward far faster than either could go alone.

"When Disney bought Pixar, John [Lasseter] and I had an intuition that we should keep the groups separate," Catmull explains. He's soft-spoken and relaxed, looking like a skinny teenager dressed up to pass for a seventy-something executive. "Steve [Jobs] thought that we'd be spreading ourselves too thin, but I had a strong philosophy on this and ultimately he listened."

A consolidation would have created plenty of efficiencies and re-duced the friction caused by running two companies and cultures at once. But Catmull had his eye on a more important creative dynamic that, he believed, dwarfed the value of corporate streamlining.

"You need to rely on intuition when you're making new things," he explains. "But how do you validate those intuitions? Let's say you have an intuition about how to solve a problem; you have to ensure that you don't become overly identified with it and resistant to it being scrutinized."

Catmull says that during the production process, his legendarily creative movie directors would quickly go from an intuition to a rigid mental structure about how things should work. If someone offered a critique, fear might grip the directors that the whole idea would unravel and the precious kernel of creativity be lost. They were afraid to analyze their intuitions, lest they turn to dust.

"Creative ideas aren't like Jenga blocks where they fall apart and you've got to start from scratch, though it can feel that way," Catmull says. "The skill of a good creative leader is being comfortable with blow-ing up an idea and knowing it will get better."

Catmull says that creatives need to hold on to the spark of intuitive insight even while it's being picked apart. This requires them to analyze their intuitions and remove the pieces that aren't fitting—often overly conventional plot points or unnecessarily complex ideas. Most creative leaders, he says, can't master this practice working all on their own; too much bias and emotion cloud their view. "What you need is an external force to hit you with a two-by-four to say it's not working."

That two-by-four came, at first, in the form of Pixar's cofounder, Steve Jobs. "Steve would come in and look at a project and say, 'I'm not a filmmaker, but I'm giving you my opinion. Take it or leave it.' He was so articulate and clear that he broke right through their resistance." Whereas Jobs was notoriously brash and offensive, Catmull is gentle and diplomatic. Partly to emulate Jobs's influence with a more posi-tive spin, Catmull created what he calls "the Brain Trust," a formalized meeting of high-level creative thinkers with very different perspectives. Designed to elicit Jobs-like clear and uncompromising feedback in a safe and supportive environment, it allowed Pixar to harness the power of intuitive creativity without allowing its directors to wall themselves off in a black box where their own biases and fear of challenge might ultimately lead them over a cliff.

So when Disney acquired Pixar in 2005, Catmull and John Lasseter saw an opportunity to create a friendly, but real, competition in which each studio would provide a two-by-four of clarity and challenge for the other. Catmull set up some basic rules for their collaborative competition. The studios would not be allowed to borrow each other's resources when they got into a pinch. They wouldn't be able to take over each other's projects. No team would have veto power over another team's movie. They were on their own to develop their cultures and philosophies. But they would have to openly share their work, and they'd have to listen to each other's criticism.

A decade after Catmull's insight that Pixar and Disney should remain separate, the approach is paying off for both studios. Catmull told me that the Disney team came in at a critical moment on Pixar's *Inside Out* and fixed some major plot problems. Then, when the Pixar team screened a cut of *Zootopia*, they saw an obvious issue. Throughout the development of that film, Nick Wilde, the fox, had been the protagonist, the problematic con artist whose arc toward redemption we follow. But the Pixar team saw that the kind rabbit, Judy Hops, really had the problem—hers was just subtler. Hops was prejudiced against predators, and it was she who had to transform. Few audience members would see themselves in a con artist, but we all can admit to having hidden prejudice. This insight was a major breakthrough for the Disney team. In 2016, *Inside Out* won the Oscar for best animated film. In 2017, *Zootopia* took the prize.

Pixar is similar to the Silicon Valley Laura Huang exposed: it is not an environment that permits analysis to trump intuition. Market research would never have guided the studio to make a film about a gourmet rat chef, a robot on a planet of trash, or the inner emotional world of a child, yet *Ratatouille*, *Wall-E*, and *Inside Out* were all breakthrough hits. Catmull's job is to keep the offbeat, intuitive insights of his writers and directors flowing freely but still open to scrutiny, tinkering, and sometimes rejection. Feel it first, then think carefully about how you feel. He says he holds himself to the same standard.

"If you think you're right 80 percent of the time, you're deluded," he says. "We need to remember we're always a lot more wrong than we thought."

Learning Environments: Wicked and Kind

As Catmull explained how he fiddles with the Pixar organizational structure and endlessly refines process and protocol, I was, at first, a little disappointed. I had expected to find a wide-ranging creative genius at the top of Pixar. Instead I had found someone who more closely resembled a visionary technocrat. Exactly what was Catmull so obsessively crafting if it wasn't the movies themselves?

A few weeks later, Robin Hogarth, the intuition researcher, provided me with an answer. Hogarth says that intuition is a learned and trainable skill. We develop intuition over time based on our experiences and the rewards and punishments we receive for using it. And that means the environments in which our intuitions develop are of critical importance. A "wicked learning environment," in Hogarth's terminology, gives us slow, ambiguous, or misleading feedback, while a "kind learning environment" gives us plenty of timely, clear, and accurate feedback. Spend a lot of time in a single environment, be it kind or wicked (most of us are blithely unaware which type of environment we're in), and we're likely to grow more and more confident in our intuition. But if our learning environments are wicked, our intuitions are likely to get further and further off base, even as they grow stronger.

Hogarth says that a wicked learning environment can lead people to draw inappropriate conclusions from successes they've had in following intuitions. "They learn the wrong rules, and if they're really successful, they start to believe their intuition gives them magical powers. The only way they learn they were wrong is by crashing. And that's a common and painful experience." The description calls to mind An Wang.

Pixar and Disney operate in a classic wicked learning environment. The studios live or die by a single product: feature-length animated films. They can produce at most two at a time, and each production takes several years. So feedback, in the form of ticket sales and critical acclaim, is painfully slow, and the sample size they learn from is tiny. A film's success or failure cannot be credited to or blamed on any particular element of the production; yet any of the thousands of elements that go into making it could potentially ruin the moviegoing experience. Through all of his behind-the-scenes machinations, Catmull is trying to convert Pixar's learning environment from a wicked one into a kind one. Opening the way for lots of direct feedback from colleagues not involved in the politics or process of the creative team is one of his strategies for doing so. When he succeeds in making the environment kind, he's giving a boost to the intuitive powers of the entire Pixar team, allowing them to confidently dream up counterintuitive hits. Catmull is responding to the simple, but little discussed, rule of human nature: Work in a wicked learning environment and our intuition can become useless, or worse, destructive. Work in a kind learning environment and our intuition becomes one of our greatest assets. How often, though, do we consciously work to make our learning environments more kind?

Hogarth's analysis also explains why venture capitalists aren't, as a group, learning to challenge their intuitions better. "Venture is an awful learning environment," laments Clint Korver, a partner at Ulu Ventures, a Silicon Valley fund. "You make one to two investments a year. The failures take two to three years. Success takes nine years. You might have made a great decision and gotten unlucky. Or vice versa. How do you learn?"

Korver, who did his PhD in decision analysis, studying under Kahneman and Tversky, is well equipped to appreciate the problem.

Hogarth has found that understanding and improving our learning environments is the most important work we can do in educating our intuition. The very notion of consciously educating our subconscious intuition may sound bizarre, but the practice isn't all that complicated.

When we form an intuitive judgment, we should ask ourselves, am I getting this intuition in a kind or wicked learning environment? If the environment is kind—that is, you've been in it long enough to understand it, it provides lots of clear and direct feedback, and it hasn't changed much over time—Hogarth says, you should be more inclined to trust it. Think back to the grandmaster and the two-dimensional chessboard. Chess is a classic kind learning environment, and chess players' intuition can indeed be enormously reliable.

If the environment is wicked, your intuition deserves a far more skeptical eye. In wicked environments, we should try to think of ways to test our intuitions before diving in. Hogarth uses the example of a waitress, Anna, who is seeking to maximize her tips but can't give maximum charm and attention to each customer. She has the hunch that well-dressed patrons will tip more, and so at peak hours, when her time is particularly tight, she focuses much more on them. Her bet seems to be confirmed, because these dapper customers do give much larger tips. So she doubles down. Her intuition is continually confirmed, and for years she follows these strategies. But Anna would benefit from considering that she has likely created the condition that the better-dressed customers tip better, because she has given them better service. What would happen, though, if she decided to check her intuition by seeking just a little bit of disconfirmatory evidence—for example, by giving her shlumpy customers attention sometimes? She might well find that, given a little more TLC, they would tip as well or maybe even better than her well-dressed customers.

If we seek disconfirming evidence or increase the volume or clarity of feedback and our intuitions hold up, this is an important sign. If they fail, we can discard them and move on with our intuitive powers slightly more honed. Again, it's a matter of listening to, but not unconditionally trusting, our guts.

Disarming Our Biases

The strategy Anna might use to hone her intuition is straightforward, but aren't the problems faced by the Silicon Valley investors more socially complex? The habit of judging people by their clothes is not as difficult to undo as that of judging them by their gender or their skin color. Indeed, a large set of studies shows that people make these kinds of prejudgments in milliseconds without even engaging their conscious minds. If it all happens so automatically, can we adjust our learning environments to make our intuitive judgments less sexist, racist, and homophobic?

Researchers Nilanjana Dasgupta and Anthony G. Greenwald knew about studies showing that attempts to reduce such biases by appealing to people's logic and reasoning skills tended to show little promise, and they wondered if they could intervene in the thought processes involved at the subconscious level. To find out, they first measured a group of white and Asian students on both their explicit racial bias against African Americans and then their subconscious implicit bias (as measured by a highly regarded diagnostic tool known as the Implicit Association Test).

After being assured that they could speak anonymously and openly, the students reported a moderate amount of conscious bias against African Americans. When tested by computer for implicit or subconscious bias, they proved a bit more negative than they'd consciously professed. Next the researchers exposed them to images of admired African Americans, like Denzel Washington and Martin Luther King Jr., and also to some despised white Americans like Jeffrey Dahmer. Nothing more was said. No arguments were made about why bias was wrong. Participants just saw silent pictures flashed on a screen.

When tested again for their level of implicit bias, the participants had moved quite significantly toward a more favorable view of African Americans in general. Twenty-four hours later, when measured again, the effect of the exposure remained. Why can just looking at a few examples that break stereotypes effect such a change? One answer might be availability bias, in which easy-to-recall examples take on disproportionate importance in our minds. The photos the participants saw became the most accessible references for their thoughts about African Americans. I found this study fascinating because it indicates that we can hack an often misleading heuristic bias to make it work in our favor. We can never hope to completely overcome availability bias, but we can consciously educate it to get smarter.

Here's one brilliant trick to do this invented by Harvard psychologist Mahzarin Banaji, who has made a career of studying unconscious bias. She installed a screensaver on her computer that flashes images of all sorts of people who counter stereotypes, such as short bald men who are executives. What might such a screensaver that flashed images of successful women entrepreneurs be worth to venture investors who can't quite intuitively grasp that many women make excellent company founders? What might it be worth to society as a whole if it spurred them to invest in more women-led companies?

When we intentionally tweak our learning environments and expose ourselves to evidence that goes against our assumptions, we can begin to separate our true intuitive insights from the junk that disguises itself as intuition. This is critical work because even the most successful intuition-driven leaders can be fooled when they fail to realize, until it's too late, that their intuition has been polluted.

But the bigger payoff goes beyond just learning to make fewer mistakes. As we hone our intuition to be more trustworthy, we can confidently devote more time to exploring ideas we have a hunch might be fruitful—but seem counterintuitive to others. Exactly this approach gave the GiveDirectly founders the confidence to push ahead with their idea even in the face of so much negative response.

Michael Faye told me about the way they pursued the idea. "We didn't want to raise too much external money, or have our livelihoods depend on it until we ourselves were convinced of the evidence of Give-Directly's impact. Once you depend on something working, you have a strong incentive to continue to tell that story—even if it's not true. We certainly didn't want that."

Having detached themselves from the outcome, Faye and his colleagues were intent on testing their intuition with hard data, and they also made that data readily available. This set them apart from most aid organizations, which traditionally don't openly share their results, partly because precise data is hard to come by and partly because there's an incentive to keep donors in the dark about outcomes. The field of development didn't even start seriously using randomized trials to inform decision making until the early 2000s, and most organizations still can't report the actual cost of an intervention.

"Donors who enjoy the warm glow of giving may be disappointed by negative results. Since that warm glow may persist if they hadn't learned the result, everyone involved may prefer avoiding careful follow-up and measurement," Faye says. Making matters worse, many small organizations will argue that they don't have money for measurement when limited funds are needed in the field. Faye doesn't buy that argument. "Imagine a drug company arguing that they were too poorly funded to test their drug, but that you should trust them and just take it. Would you take that pill?"

These practices of lax measurement and reporting, of course, create a wicked learning environment in which the intuition of donors and aid agencies alike is confirmed when it should be challenged. GiveDirectly's founders, on the other hand, fanatically lined up outside evaluators to watch them every step of the way, reporting the good and the bad. They incubated their idea in as kind a learning environment as they could create. Just as Ed Catmull discovered with his teams at Pixar and Disney, doing so fueled their creative drive. "One of the most important things evidence gave us in the early days was the fortitude to keep going," Faye told me. "When people told me I was wrong, I went back to the evidence and was reassured."

An intuitive insight used as a hypothesis. Plenty of science and a commitment to learning, giving bias less fertile ground in which to flourish. Had the intuition of GiveDirectly's founders been mere false pattern recognition, they would have known early on before their livelihoods depended on it. But their rigorous observations confirmed that the pattern was real—and changed the intuition of an entire field.

This mix of intuition and analysis can help overcome our biases and more effectively spot counterintuitive breakthroughs. But one more piece is still missing in our search to understand intuition and counterintuition. How do we generate powerful counterintuitive ideas to begin with? We'll untangle that question next.

CHAPTER 9

Leaping into the Counterintuitive

*How to tackle difficult problems
with unexpected solutions*

By 1994, Bogotá, Colombia, had earned a reputation as one of the most dangerous and difficult cities to live in on the planet. Its 4,200 homicides the previous year made it the world's murder capital. Its buildings were crumbling as money meant for public works routinely got funneled to corrupt government officials, to be dropped into bank accounts already overflowing with "donations" from drug cartels. In a city with little to take pride in or hope for, and where the authorities were as dangerous as the criminals, citizens regularly flouted the law; they abused public spaces and each other.

Angry about a future with no prospects, frustrated students at Bogotá's largest university began to gather and lash out. One night, 2,000 of them assembled in a campus auditorium. The packed room was loud and chaotic and, to many there, seemed on the verge of violence.

And then this: The university president appears on the stage, and, predictably, the students erupt in angry jeers. The shaggy-haired man, wearing professorial glasses and an Abe Lincoln–style beard, looks frightened and dismayed. Though he stands behind a microphone, it's highly doubtful that he'll be heard over the roaring crowd. And even if he is, there's little he can say to address the students' rage. What can he promise them? A new, functional society? So, he says nothing. Instead, he walks slowly toward the students, loosens his belt, turns around, and drops his pants to his ankles. He bends forward, naked from the waist down, and the room falls into stunned silence. This isn't a flash. It's a prolonged and, I'm sorry to say, spread-cheeked display. Rage turns to laughter, and amazingly the assembly ends peacefully.

Antanas Mockus later claims that he wanted to show the students "the color of peace—white." The explanation does little to save his academic career. Despite his newfound popularity with the university's students, he's promptly forced to resign. But Mockus's story is just beginning.

Whereas the university officials see the act as an outrage, Mockus, a philosophy and mathematics professor, sees the whole incident as powerful proof of a theory he'd long been formulating. Many culturally intuitive notions of what drives human behavior are two-dimensional and insufficient, he believes. We can coerce, threaten, and incentivize people all we want, but when they have lost faith in their leaders (and perhaps even when they haven't), such tactics will have limited impact. What's actually needed, Mockus believes, is to grab their attention, interrupt their expectations, change the story they think they're in, and then give them agency to act out a new script if they see fit.

"What people love most is when you write on the blackboard a risky first half of a sentence and then recognize their freedom to write the other half," Mockus would later say.

Yes, Mockus has made a fool of himself, but he's also managed to depressurize a situation that was near bursting and had no obvious release valve. Excited by this first, perhaps questionable victory, Mockus decides to test his theory on a much larger stage, to turn the city of Bogotá itself into one enormous experiment.

A few months later, out of a makeshift office in his mother's home, the Mockus for Mayor campaign is in full swing. The mooning stunt has established him as the ultimate political outsider, and for a populace with zero confidence in business as usual, he makes for an appealing protest vote. The soft-spoken independent candidate manages to evolve beyond the archetype of a clown, making promises to bring pride and respect back to the city. Mockus wins the election by the widest margin of any Bogotá mayoral candidate in history.

Thus begins what is known as Bogotá's "invasion of the intellectuals." Mockus brings in an administration of social scientists and statisticians all tasked with engaging the citizenry in a grand project to beautify, revitalize, and reduce violence and criminality within the city. In some ways, Mockus sounds like a "law and order" mayor, but his approach has nothing to do with prisons, increased police presence, and stricter rules. In fact, quite the opposite. Everything Mockus does will be far more counterintuitive.

Let's start on the streets. One of the most demoralizing and dangerous aspects of life in Bogotá is the lawless traffic. Drivers disregard basic rules and pedestrians with impunity. Pedestrians return the favor, ignoring signals and slowing traffic to a standstill. This is, in large part, because the city's thousands of traffic police are outrageously corrupt. They spend far more time shaking drivers down than enforcing laws and civility. Mockus hypothesizes that Bogotá's drivers and pedestrians aren't inherently bad. They just see no reason to comply with the rules when the rule enforcers are bullies.

So he trains several dozen traffic mimes. These young people fan out around the city to playfully mock bad drivers and disrespectful pedestrians. A crowd celebrates one mime as he tries, in cartoonish futility, to push a bus out of a crosswalk. Another mime shadows a man wandering dangerously through traffic, mimicking his every move. A group of pedestrians roars their approval. Then Mockus lets everyone in on the game, distributing hundreds of thousands of white cards with a thumbs-up symbol and red cards with a thumbs-down symbol. Soon pedestrians and drivers are thanking each other for good behavior and shaming each other for bad.

Replacing cops with mimes and red cards sounds absurd until we understand the hidden logic: whereas citizens care nothing about behaving well for cops, they do care about behaving well for each other. In a matter of months, the number of pedestrians obeying traffic signals triples to 75 percent. Traffic accidents and commute times plummet. The program is so successful that Mockus fires all 3,200 Bogotá traffic cops. Four hundred of them accept his offer to return to the force as mimes.

As Mockus's intellectuals analyze the violence epidemic, they pinpoint what they believe to be the source of the problem. Colombian home life is violent, in subtle and not so subtle ways, and this everyday violence spills out into the streets, leading to fighting, kidnapping, and often murder. For an administration that promises to fight crime, this is a surprisingly empathetic view of offenders, and this formulation of the problem leads to some extremely unconventional interventions.

Mockus goes on television and shares that he was abused as a young child. Then he draws the face of his abuser on a balloon and punches it. He asks the city's residents, who by now have a bewildered respect for their mayor, to try committing their own symbolic acts of violence rather than physical ones. Next, he hosts a call-in television show in which children report the abuse happening in their own homes. Their stories begin to denormalize beatings, threats, and intimidation of children. Police go to school to study nonviolent conflict resolution. When asked by his security team to wear a bulletproof vest, Mockus cuts a heart-shaped hole in the chest. All of these actions, Mockus explains, aim to create a new taboo against violence in a city that's somehow come to casually accept it.

The mayor's office rolls out one unexpected attack on the city's woes after the next. It levies a "voluntary tax," asking citizens to donate 10 percent of their income to the city; 65,000 comply. Mockus dresses up as a superhero to collect litter and makes a public service announcement featuring himself naked in the shower to encourage people to save water.

By the time he leaves office, Bogotá has become one of the safest, cleanest cities in the region. The murder rate has fallen by 70 percent. Every home has electricity, sewer service, and running water. City revenues are up 30 percent, and much of that money goes to building or revitalizing city parks—public spaces that citizens will now take care of. Corruption is no longer a part of everyday life. Ninety-nine percent of children attend school.

It all began with an outrageous act committed by a man who saw the world differently and was willing to risk it all for his beliefs.

Governments and businesses around the world spend a great deal of time and money trying to pull the obvious levers of human behavior. We construct rewards and punishments with the assumption that people behave in their economic best interests, even though behavioral economists have shattered that notion in recent decades, demonstrating how emotionally driven, irrational, and nonselfish we can often be. We create marketing campaigns to persuade people to change their views, even though a large body of research on a phenomenon known as the "backlash effect" shows that directly challenging people's beliefs usually makes them dig in further. These well-understood insights into human psychology explain why so many seemingly obvious solutions don't work as hoped, such as imposing stricter criminal sentencing, raising water prices in a drought, and creating billboards warning of the dangers of climate change.

Recognizing that all this effort is wasted can be depressing. Accepting the brokenness of seemingly obvious ways of thinking can leave us feeling hopeless, so instead many of us just press on with mediocre solutions. Mockus's genius, as befitted a philosopher and a man of science, was not only to accept that humans are more complicated than they seem but to search for new levers to pull that would work. He turned his attention to stimulating people's imagination, conscience, and inherent desire to feel part of their community. This opened up a world of possibilities.

Mockus's story illustrates how counterintuitive insights need not come from the mysterious visions of the mad (though the mooning incident does show the mayor possessed a tinge of madness). Rather, they can grow logically from stepping back, finding those places where conventional thinking is broken, and then creatively attacking the problem from a new angle. To do that, however, we must begin with a willingness to work through the discomfort of accepting that some of our most basic beliefs about how the world works might be leading us astray. That, it turns out, doesn't come easily to most.

Embracing the Absurd

Four years before Antanas Mockus showed students the color of peace, Marilyn vos Savant famously received a question by mail that would set off nearly as much outrage.

Savant was used to difficult questions, so she didn't think much of this one when it first arrived in her mailbox along with dozens of others.

In 1988, the *Guinness Book of World Records* had proclaimed her to have the highest IQ ever recorded. If you're wondering if Savant (meaning "one who knows") is some sort of arrogant stage name inspired by the honor, it's not. Genius must just go way back in her family. Savant leveraged her newfound fame to create a column in *Parade* magazine, *Ask Marilyn*, in which "the world's smartest human" solves particularly thorny logic puzzles sent in by readers.

In September 1990, Craig F. Whitaker asked Savant the following question:

> Suppose you're on a game show, and you're given the choice of three doors. Behind one door is a car, behind the others, goats. You pick a door, say #1, and the host, who knows what's behind the doors, opens another door, say #3, which has a goat. He says to you, "Do you want to pick door #2?" Is it to your advantage to switch your choice of doors?

Whitaker's question is known as the Monty Hall problem, a puzzle familiar to those who enjoy such brain benders but, up until then, unknown to the general public. Savant believed she had the answer: you should switch. Your chances of winning if you do, she asserted, are 66 percent. If you stick with your original choice, your chances are only 33 percent.

Here's how she explained the logic to her readers:

> Suppose there are a million doors, and you pick door #1. Then the host, who knows what's behind the doors and will always avoid the one with the prize, opens them all except door #777,777. You'd switch to that door pretty fast, wouldn't you?

She thought that might settle it, but even the smartest person in the world can be wrong sometimes.

If you've never seen the Monty Hall problem before, your brain might hurt when you hear Savant claim you can raise your chances significantly by switching. It just seems obvious that there's no difference between sticking with your choice and switching. You might even feel a bit of outrage at Savant's suggestion. That's exactly what thousands of her readers felt—not just disagreement but outright anger and hostility. She received thousands of letters about this single column.

"You blew it!" wrote Robert Sachs of George Mason University. "As a professional mathematician, I'm very concerned about the general public's lack of mathematical skills. Please help by confessing your error and in the future being more careful."

"There is enough mathematical illiteracy in this country, and we don't need the world's highest IQ propagating more. Shame!" was the response of an enraged Scott Smith of the University of Florida.

Savant said that 92 percent of the letters she received told her she was wrong. Two-thirds of the letters she received from universities lectured her on her error. Searching to reconcile the fact that she was a genius with their conviction that she had flubbed a simple problem, her detractors offered explanations such as "Maybe women look at math problems different from men." She was told she was wrong by the director of the Center of Defense Information and a mathematical statistician from the National Institutes of Health.

Wrote Everett Harman from the US Army Research Institute, "You made a mistake, but look at the positive side. If all those Ph.D.'s were wrong, the country would be in some very serious trouble."

Except they *were* wrong. Savant was right.

Let's look at the math (though many of Savant's readers weren't convinced until she suggested they simply run the game a few dozen times themselves to see that switching really does work). Intuitively it makes sense that picking the correct door is random chance on the first guess, and when asked if you want to switch your guess, it's random chance again. It shouldn't matter. But an important piece of information is almost invisible on first reading: the host knows what's behind the doors. That means regardless of what you choose, the host will never show you a car. Suddenly the puzzle isn't so random after all. Still, that doesn't clarify why you should switch.

So let's run through the scenarios. What are the chances you chose right on the first guess? One in three, right? And if you chose correctly, you shouldn't switch. If you do, you'll lose. But if you chose wrong (a two out of three chance), the host, by showing you which alternative door not to pick, has just guaranteed that you will win if you do switch! Don't switch and your chances of winning are 33 percent. Switch and your chances are 66 percent. If this still doesn't make sense, I, like Savant, suggest you play it out twenty times with two black cards (the goats), a red card (the car), and a friend willing to act as the host.

By 1992, Savant had had thousands of classrooms run the game. Researchers even built computer models to run the experiment millions of times. The outcome: switch and you win 66 percent of the time. Still, faced with this evidence, the 8 percent of readers who accepted her answer grew to only 56 percent, and even among academics, acceptance hovered around 71 percent. The puzzle defies how the world seems to work, and confronted with this affront to our intuition, most of us search desperately to resolve our discomfort. Academics waved their credentials as if this in any way refuted the logic. Men blamed the disconnect on feminine incompetence. Some readers, in the face of all the numeric evidence, simply said that they chose not to believe it.

Why all the outrage? Why the convoluted and irrelevant evidence marshaled to refute Savant? Because, for anyone willing to sit with it for a moment, this puzzle induces cognitive dissonance: the experience of holding two opposing ideas at once. Our intuition tells us clearly that there simply cannot be an advantage in switching. The world's smartest human, computer models, and (if we're willing to run the experiment) experience ask us to believe otherwise.

When confronted with cognitive dissonance, we naturally try to resolve it immediately. The brain may get angry and lash out. Another automatic tactic is to resolve dissonance through "logic" that looks absurd to an outside observer. For instance, psychologists have studied apocalyptic cults to see what happens when specifically dated prophecies of doom don't come to pass. Do the cult members quit the cult when the day the world will end comes and goes without incident? Some do, but most double down in their belief. They construct logic like "The world would have ended, but God changed his mind because we believed." And they happily press on, more committed than ever and no longer holding two beliefs at once. They have conveniently discarded the possibility that the prophecy was wrong.

"Faced with the choice of changing one's mind and proving that there's no need to do so, almost everyone gets busy on the proof," wrote economist John Kenneth Galbraith.

Embracing cognitive dissonance, while uncomfortable, is actually quite a good thing. When exposed to things that don't work as we assume, instead of grasping for quick resolution and often opting to retreat into more pleasing thoughts, we can greet this information as fuel for creative insight.

Working patiently with brain-bending information takes effort. Zen monks spend long periods with koans—or unresolvable riddles—to train themselves to accept the unpleasantness of not being able to find easy answers or simply to turn their attention elsewhere. While such practice might seem an abstract luxury, Albert Einstein did just this to develop some of the most important and counterintuitive scientific ideas the world has known.

Even as a teenager, Einstein loved playing with paradoxes. He called the ideas he tested in his mind, rather than a lab, thought experiments. His first breakthrough from this kind of game came at the age of sixteen.

He had recently run away from a school that insisted on rote memorization and enrolled at a village school that taught students to visualize concepts. This led him to wonder what it would look like to travel alongside a light beam, if he himself were moving at the speed of light.

To understand what he visualized, think of two trains traveling next to each other in the same direction and at the same speed. If you can't see the landscape beyond the other train zooming along, the other train appears not to be moving at all. Einstein inferred from this that if he were traveling on a light beam and looked over at another light beam moving in the same direction, it would appear to be at rest. But physicists already knew that this was not possible. According to Maxwell's equations, which describe the motion of magnetic fields, regardless of the movement of an observer, light will always appear to travel at, well, the speed of light. Einstein accepted that unlike in the train scenario, traveling at the speed of light next to a light beam would not cause that beam to appear to stand still. But how could that be?

Einstein said this thought experiment caused him a "psychic tension," and he wandered around for days, palms sweating. For most of us, this would be a good moment to turn to simpler, less troubling thoughts, but Einstein said immersing himself in the paradox was one of the most pleasant experiences of his life.

He later claimed that this question contained the germ of his theory of special relativity, which states that time is relative and even that space and time are part of the same phenomenon. He wrote, "All attempts to clarify this paradox satisfactorily were condemned to failure as long as the axiom of the absolute character of time . . . was rooted unrecognized in the unconscious. To recognize clearly this axiom and its arbitrary character already implies the essential solution."

In other words, we intuitively sense time as a fixed reality. How could we not, spending our entire existence on this little spinning globe where time always behaves as it should? But set that assumption aside for a moment, and you can answer the riddle of why, when riding at the speed of light next to a light beam, that light beam will still appear to be moving. Time, for you, has slowed down to a standstill. To grasp this, imagine yourself on that train again. Time for you, but only for you, slows down. The other train, moving at its constant speed, will appear to be moving. Don't worry if this new understanding of time that Einstein pioneered still isn't intuitive. It's one of those insights that never loses its mind-bending character. It took decades for Einstein to convince the world of this insanely counterintuitive nature of the universe, but experiment after experiment proved him right.

If Einstein hadn't enjoyed letting his mind engage in paradox, leading him to such wildly counterintuitive notions, and felt enough comfort to sit with the cognitive dissonance that caused him, we might not have GPS, television, or radar, to name just a few aspects of modern life his relativity theories made possible (not to mention the revolution in physics his insights sparked).

I'm not suggesting, of course, that enjoying cognitive dissonance will make us all Einsteins. We don't need to be. If you look under the hood of many ingenious counterintuitive breakthroughs, you'll find rather ordinary people who have moved toward, rather than run from, a seeming paradox and found a pathway to resolving it. Such thinking is being used right now, in fact, to revolutionize America's most popular sport.

Unsafe Thinking About Safety

When Kenney Bui was six years old, he wandered into the living room where his father, Ngon Bui, sat, leaning raptly toward the family television. The young boy climbed into his father's lap.

"What is this thing, Dad?" he asked, interested because the man he idolized was so interested.

"Football, Kenney," his father replied.

Kenney had endless questions for Ngon, who tried to answer without losing focus on the game. Who's winning? Are they allowed to do that? What team are you rooting for?

Ngon Bui was an avid Seattle Seahawks fan. He had left Vietnam in 1975 and arrived in his adopted American city confused and unprepared. The Seahawks would arrive in similar fashion a year later, and Ngon had felt a kinship and a love for the team ever since.

"I like the Seahawks," he told Kenney with some understatement.

"OK, you love the Seahawks?" Kenney said. "I love the Seahawks too."

Thus began a lifelong fascination with football for Kenney Bui. He made friends easily and just as gracefully maintained a 4.0 grade point average through high school. But even though he was a slight 5'8" and 150 pounds, Kenney lived for football. Like his hero, NFL safety Earl Thomas, Kenney overcame his small size as a defensive back by playing with an extra level of ferocity and putting punishing hits on opposing receivers.

On October 2, 2015, Ngon Bui was working late, so as usual he would be missing the chance to watch his son play for Evergreen High School. Part of him regretted it, but part of him, if he was honest, was relieved not to be there. A month earlier, Kenney had been removed from a game with a mild concussion. Ngon got so scared, he told Kenney it was time he stopped playing the game they both loved. He tried not to sign the school form acknowledging the concussion, a form that would let Kenney back onto the field, but his son wouldn't give up.

Across town, the game against Highline had entered the fourth quarter. Kenney was a senior. His prospects for playing college ball weren't high, and he knew he probably wouldn't have that many more chances for on-field heroics. He was determined to make every hit count. So when a short pass gave Kenney an open shot at a Highline receiver, he lowered his head and hit his opponent like Earl Thomas would. Hard.

Then Kenney walked slowly to the sidelines and sat down. He closed his eyes as the worried trainers asked him standard questions from the concussion protocol. He would go straight from the bench to Harborview Medical Center, where he would lie unconscious for the next three days until life support was removed. Kenney would become one of nineteen American students to die playing football in 2015.

Shortly after Kenney's death, Ngon received a package from Seahawks coach Pete Carrol. Ngon reached inside and pulled out a jersey. Number 29, Earl Thomas, signed by Kenney's hero himself.

"I want to keep that," Ngon told a reporter from the *Guardian*. "And I want to wear that jersey so every time I wear it I think of Kenney. My favorite son."

That Ngon Bui should cherish this jersey, an artifact representing a player whom his son died trying to emulate, reflects a larger crisis in American culture. Many feel we can no longer watch our children destroy their bodies and brains for a game. At the same time, it seems we can't stop watching football. The only solution is to somehow make the game safer. But how? That question has been particularly bedeviling. In fact, until Erik Swartz, a kinesiologist at the University of New Hampshire (UNH), began developing a counterintuitive solution, football reformers had hit one dead end after another.

Football has always been a dangerous sport. As the game began to reach national prominence in the 1960s and players got stronger, faster, and more determined to achieve fame, the number of deaths from brain injuries began to climb from already unacceptably high levels. Between 1965 and 1969, more than one hundred players died; that's a rate of about twenty per year.

At the University of Michigan, neuroscientist Richard Schneider decided there might be a simple solution to this problem: improve the protective quality of helmets. "For decades, the intuitive logical approach has been: we have head injuries so let's put a helmet on," Swartz, the UNH kinesiologist, told me. "This body part is getting hurt. Let's put something over it to protect it and problem solved."

By the end of the 1960s, Schneider had radically reengineered football helmets to have far more padding, better resist shock, and be more comfortable. Like a good scientist he also carefully observed game footage to spot the styles of play most likely to cause brain injury. He proposed a few minor rule changes to ban the most dangerous head-first maneuvers, like spearing and butt blocking. The rule changes essentially meant that you couldn't use your helmet or face mask to punish an opponent.

Schneider's work had an immediate and enormous impact. By 1973, head-injury fatalities in high schools had dropped by three-quarters. Too many kids were still dying, but we seemed well on our way to saving football players and the game itself.

At the time, however, Schneider and the rest of the world didn't know that improved helmets weren't solving the kind of problem that would kill Kenney Bui. In fact, they were making the problem worse. Concussions occur when a collision with the head causes the brain to knock into the internal walls of the skull. Even with relatively light impact, this leads to brain swelling and cumulative damage as one concussion follows another. Second-impact syndrome, which likely killed Kenney Bui, can happen suddenly when a second concussion occurs before the swelling has receded from an earlier one. It has a 75 percent fatality rate. So how are better helmets making the concussion problem worse?

"It's called risk homeostasis," Swartz says. "It's that false sense of security you get when you think you're protected. So you take more chances. You act more recklessly." As helmets have gotten ever bigger and more comfortable, players have felt safe within these technological cocoons. An estimated 70 percent of high school players with concussions continue to play. And playing usually means, even for highly intelligent kids like Kenney Bui, using their heads as a weapon.

"It's just not natural to take your head and drive it into a solid surface. But helmets make it seem fine," Swartz says. In fact, he says, players have become so comfortable with collisions that head butts have replaced high fives. "This can add another twenty impacts a day," he laments.

Still, who can imagine going back to helmet-less football? Players and fans would either have to deal with gruesome on-field injuries— broken necks, open head wounds—or the game would have to slow down and become far more measured, almost certainly destroying the entertainment value of the sport. So most of us throw our hands up, either forbidding our children to play and turning away from the game or, more likely, putting the reality that football is a blood sport out of our minds long enough to enjoy the bone-crunching hard hits and on-field heroics.

Erik Swartz began to untangle the problem, however, much as we might untangle the Monty Hall problem or as Einstein began to un-tangle time, by sitting with the discomfort that the world doesn't work how we might intuitively expect it to, embracing that reality, and then thinking of a logical path forward.

So here was the problem Swartz faced: football will always be played with helmets, but helmets make players more prone to concussion. It's like a koan, an unsolvable riddle.

It doesn't have to be, Swartz discovered, if you reframe the problem. Helmets do not make players more prone to concussion; their behavior while wearing helmets does. Suddenly a fact of nature becomes a problem of human psychology. And with this insight, Swartz saw a glimmer of daylight toward which he could run.

Swartz went to the UNH coaching staff with a bold and strange proposal. He wanted to create an experimental group on the school's team and train them differently. In drills, they would practice with their helmets off. The plan seemed outrageous at first to head coach Sean McDonnell. Coaches commonly yell at players at all levels for taking their helmets off even when standing injured on the side-lines. Wearing a helmet is just part of team discipline. And players who practiced without helmets might be at a distinct disadvantage on game day. They might learn to play soft. Still, Swartz's logic made a kind of odd sense to McDonnell, who had lost too many players to concussions over the years. So he allowed Swartz to recruit a set of volunteers for his study.

One of those volunteers, Daniel Rowe, had started wondering if he should be playing football at all. He had sustained three concussions in three years and was unlikely to go pro. He thought logically he shouldn't go on playing but was reluctant to quit. So he figured practicing without his helmet was worth a shot.

"When you take the helmet off, you're highly conscious, like 'I can't get a scratch.' You don't want to do anything damaging above the shoulders," Rowe recalled. The hundreds of tackling drills he did without a helmet retrained him to lead with other parts of his body and to keep his head well out of the way of impact. That season, Rowe was concussion-free, and the safer style of play made him more comfortable during games, leading to what he says was his best season in terms of on-field performance.

"I felt much safer, and I left games feeling more confident about my health," he said. "It took away the factor of, 'Am I okay? Or am I not okay?'"

Swartz's data show that the program has improved overall tackling performance on UNH's team, while the players in his experimental group experienced 28 percent fewer head impacts. These are impressive results for a single-season intervention but only a glimmer of the potential impact on the sport if kids start practicing without helmets in youth leagues, when their habits are forming, and eventually play consistently against opponents who have been trained to protect their heads.

In 2016, the Seattle Seahawks, the team Kenney and Ngon so loved, began implementing Swartz's program.

Swartz says that NFL players will likely suffer the catastrophic effects of concussions for a couple more decades, but he has a lot of hope that we can train today's generation of youth players and coaches to think of players' heads as precious and fragile, not as indestructible weapons.

The idea of improving player safety by removing helmets during practice is completely counterintuitive—so much so, in fact, that while experts argued endlessly about solutions that would never see the light of day, like banning football in high school, implementing complicated rule changes, and removing helmets altogether from the game, nobody had ever studied this straightforward approach. Yet Swartz found a simple and effective solution.

How to Cultivate Counterintuitive Creativity

When I set out to probe into the nature of counterintuitive insights, which I believed were some of the purest expressions of unsafe thinking, I figured I'd find a truly wild type of creativity at work. I was wrong. Those I talked to and read about who had pursued such insights came across as rather normal people for whom entertaining counterintuitive ideas seemed natural. When asked how they came up with such counterintuitive notions, many seemed surprised by the question. Once they had examined a seemingly intractable situation from a number of angles, pressing on beyond surface appearances and obvious paths forward, a perfectly logical and sane-seeming path forward opened up. These paths didn't present themselves as counterintuitive at all, though to those stuck in old ways of thinking, they appeared to be just that. Headlines about GiveDirectly, Mockus, and Swartz marveled at the wackiness of their approaches. But that's not at all how they looked to their creators. Hearing their stories, I realized that I was observing a set of straightforward practices we all can use to create counterintuitive breakthroughs ourselves. We can use a set of established tools to optimize our ability to entertain more seemingly outlandish ideas. We need not wait for lightning to strike but rather can cultivate counterintuitive thinking.

Here's how.

Embrace Cognitive Dissonance

As we've just seen, counterintuitive solutions often begin with accepting that the world doesn't work in the ways we'd intuitively expect it to. It's so easy to sweep these realities under the rug and press on as if our assumptions were right. If we want to break out of ruts, however, we need to move toward this information, to learn to enjoy it as Einstein did. Here are a few long-established counterintuitive facts that rarely get acted on: More homework does not increase student performance and often decreases it. Building more traffic lanes often makes traffic worse. Trying to convince people that they are wrong, especially about a moral belief, usually entrenches them deeper in their original position. None of this means we should stop trying to improve student performance, ease traffic congestion, or change minds. But it does mean that we're wasting a lot of time and money by ignoring reality—and that there is enormous opportunity in embracing it.

What are the inconvenient truths of your industry or your company? You might ask questions like the following to discover them:

- What do our most persistent critics or unhappy customers say about us, and what's the grain of truth therein? How might we finally address their seemingly intractable concerns?

- What do we say we do (in our mission or core values statements) but never actually get around to because we're sure it's too expensive or difficult?

- Does our strategy actually align with the latest science about how people behave, communicate, and get persuaded?

Think of the inconvenient truths you dig up as starting points for engaging in productive cognitive dissonance rather than as obstacles to avoid.

Reformulate the Problem

Moving toward the kinds of thorny problems that induce cognitive dissonance presents an obvious pitfall. These problems can appear to have no solution at all, which is why they remain unsolved. That was the case with the conundrum Swartz faced that helmets are both indispensable and extremely dangerous. Here Einstein again offers an important mind-set and approach: "If I had an hour to solve a problem and my life depended on the solution," he wrote, "I would spend the first fifty-five minutes determining the proper question to ask, for once I know the proper question, I could solve the problem in less than five minutes." Swartz reformulated the question as "How can we keep helmets in the sport but get rid of the dangerous behavior they encourage?" This was a nut he could crack.

Before spending any more time trying to solve a particularly difficult problem, ask if you *must* solve it to reach the end you're seeking.
Might you solve other problems instead that will achieve the same result? Might subtle reformulations of the problem open new doors?

Bring in an Outsider's Mind-set, or Simply an Outsider

The counterintuitive thinkers I encountered owed a large part of their
success to their outsider status. Swartz, a rugby player, observed that
players in his sport hardly ever used their heads when tackling, making
it obvious to him that players could be safe, at least part of the time, on
the field without helmets. The GiveDirectly founders were economists
dabbling in foreign aid. Mockus was an academic masquerading as a
politician. The intuitive to these outsiders was counterintuitive, and ingenious, within their fields.

Just as the army brought Abraham Wald, a statistician, in to help
with the problem of protecting bombers and reaped an important
counterintuitive insight as a result, we can all benefit from inviting outsiders into our solution finding or leveraging our own knowledge from
other, unrelated fields.

Listen to, Then Test Intuition

The practices we've looked at so far help to set the conditions for more
creative solutions to emerge, and they largely engage our rational, analytic thinking systems. Once the conditions are in place, however, we
need to employ a healthy dose of open and creative thinking. In the
case of GiveDirectly, that creativity simply combined preexisting ideas:
direct cash transfers and digital payments. There was nothing flashy
about it. Bogotá's mayor Antanas Mockus, on the other hand, leaned on
a far more radical and theatrical approach. He responded to his understanding of human nature with an extremely unsafe offbeat artistry that
arose from his intuition about what might shake citizens loose from their
thought patterns. But even with such an iconoclastic approach, Mockus
leaned heavily on that marriage of intuition and analysis discussed in

the last chapter. Here's how he described one of the key lessons from his time in politics: "It helps to develop short, pleasing experiences for people that generate stories of delightful surprise, moments of mutual admiration among citizens and the welcome challenge of understanding something new. But then you need to consolidate those stories with good statistical results obtained through cold, rational measurement. That creates a virtuous cycle, so that congenial new experiences lead to statistically documented improvements, and the documentation raises expectations for more welcome change."

We should not dismiss counterintuitive approaches simply because they defy conventional wisdom. We should capture them as they appear in our creative processes, even when they come from our own mysterious intuitive thinking. Once they do emerge, we must then test them rigorously. Counterintuitive insights hold great promise because they are so rarely tried. That doesn't mean they're always right.

Present Ideas as Minimally Counterintuitive

In terms of gaining acceptance from our customers, team members, and bosses, without which they will never take root, counterintuitive concepts have both inherent advantages and significant disadvantages. Eli Pariser is cofounder of Upworthy, a website that built a user base of hundreds of millions by optimizing story headlines to draw in user attention. He's tested every possible attention-getting strategy millions of times over. He told me that counterintuitive ideas absolutely draw attention. Unexpected scientific findings, surprising propositions, and weird pairings tend to delight and arouse curiosity. But there can be too much of a good thing. Counterintuitive concepts, when they break too many expectations and arouse too much dissonance, are often automatically dismissed or ignored.

An interesting body of research demonstrates that people tend to tune in to, remember, and talk about ideas that strike a happy medium. Known as minimally counterintuitive concepts, they tend to be rather mundane in most ways but to have one or two features that break expectations. We see them everywhere in legends and stories that have survived for centuries. Ghosts mostly behave as we expect humans to but can pass through solid matter and are no longer alive. A virgin mother doesn't fly, flit in and out of existence, or magically transform into an animal; she is like any other mother except that she conceived without intercourse. Aliens fly in metal spaceships and generally have two eyes, a nose, and a mouth; they just happen to come from other planets. Laboratory studies have repeatedly shown that an entirely intuitive concept is easily overlooked. A concept that is too counterintuitive is difficult to recall or understand at all.

What are the implications for our own counterintuitive ideas? It is often best to present them as a twist on already well-understood ways of doing things. Airbnb launched as AirBedandBreakfast, emphasizing that people all around the world were already opening their homes to strangers by running bed-and-breakfasts. Early Airbnb hosts were nothing at all like professional bed-and-breakfast owners, but the analogy made the new model feel safer and better established in renters' minds. Not until the platform had redefined cultural intuition about the hospitality business could the analogy be forgotten, though of course it persists to this day in the name. As you present your counterintuitive ideas, emphasize just how conventional most, but not all, of their elements are. They are much more likely to gain support and acceptance.

This process of questioning culturally unquestioned notions, developing intuitions that diverge from conventional approaches, and then testing the radical but rational solutions that emerge is core to unsafe thinking. We've looked deeply at how to strengthen our minds to embrace and press on with these kinds of counterconventional approaches. But we must also acknowledge that the world is often hostile to them and can discourage us at every turn. Endless rules exist to protect and preserve status quo thinking—whole moral structures that discourage rocking the boat. Stepping away from normal ways of operating, we will necessarily crash headlong into them. How do we do so effectively, without getting rejected as outlaws? And how do we confront our own desire to do what we've been told is the right thing when we know the right thing is no longer good enough? I searched for those answers next.

FLEXIBILITY: KEY TAKEAWAYS

Pay attention to your intuitions . . .

In an age of data and analysis, intuition rarely gets credit for the genius it holds (though privately most executives do admit it's an indispensable tool). Intuitions can't be justified through step-by-step logic, and they often come to us as emotions and bodily feelings rather than ideas. That makes intuition easy to dismiss. We can elevate it back to its rightful place by making a specific commitment to openly discussing and taking advantage of intuition.

Do you intentionally tune in to how you feel about ideas and decisions rather than simply what you think about them? Do you encourage others to share their gut feelings without immediately asking them to explain why? The more you gather intuitive ideas and responses from yourself and your team, the more genius you'll have access to.

. . . But don't trust them blindly

Intuitions aren't truths. They are interesting hypotheses, or as Robin Hogarth says, "they are data that need to be explained." Test your intuitions because they are so often polluted by bias and fast thinking shortcuts. Creating a "kind learning environment" with plenty of feedback and data has been the key for Pixar, GiveDirectly, and the city of Bogotá in leading intuition-inspired revolutions.

Can you identify whether you operate in a kind or wicked learning environment? What steps can you take to make your learning environment kinder with better feedback, more data, and less bias built into the system?

Chip away at your biases

Remember the simple but effective trick of using a screensaver with short, bald executives and other people who defied stereotypes?

What do you do to remind yourself that neat boxes rarely describe reality? Do you ever intentionally seek out evidence that undermines your basic assumptions?

(continues)

Embrace the difficult and the absurd

We find the most fodder for creativity in the problems that seem intractable and that we wish to quickly resolve with simple solutions. Stick with these problems longer than is comfortable (remember Einstein wandering around with sweating palms?). Reframe them as Erik Swartz did (the problem is not helmets but the behavior of people wearing them). And open the space to entertain outlandish solutions (if traffic mimes can outperform cops, anything is possible).

If you've got well-crafted, honed intuition, you'll have a good shot at separating out the good solutions from the dumb ones. This is how ideas, intuitive to just a few, can become counterintuitive breakthroughs that change the world.

PART 5

MORALITY

CHAPTER 10

When Wrong Is Right

*Why being creative sometimes means
bending (or breaking) the rules*

Marissa Mayer didn't just dislike the idea. She thought it was downright creepy. Yet there was something creepily brilliant about what Paul Buchheit had just suggested.

For years, Buchheit had been working on a skunkworks project to create a new service known internally as Caribou. A few in the company's leadership were already using a prototype version of the service, and it worked well, but the effort had stalled because the company couldn't figure out how to make it pay for itself—in the hands of the public it could potentially drain billions from Google's coffers.

Buchheit had come up with a solution, but it looked pretty devious—which was ironic because Buchheit had been the one to suggest Google's now famous motto "Don't be evil."

The service ultimately came to be known as Gmail, and Buchheit had proposed that it could cover the cost of providing a free gigabyte of storage and even earn serious revenue by reading incoming emails and then serving up ads that would butt in on the conversation, like a socially inept, half-drunk cocktail party attendee.

Your friend: Want to grab dinner tonight?
You: Sure. Where?
Weird guy who's been listening in: Try the new giant buffalo wings bucket for only $19.99.

Creepy. Mayer was sure of it. "It's going to be terrible," she remembers thinking. She told Buchheit the idea was a no-go. At the end of the meeting, Mayer put a fine point on the kabash.

"When I walked out the door, I stopped for a minute," she later recalled. "And I said, 'So Paul, we agreed we are not exploring the whole ad thing now, right? And he was like, 'Yup, right.'"

The promise sounded sincere but lasted only a couple of hours. Buchheit was so certain that seeing the ads served up would change his boss's mind that he worked like mad that night building the feature. The next morning, when Mayer checked her email, she saw that a friend had invited her to go hiking, and next to the message appeared an ad for hiking boots. Next, she viewed an invitation to see Al Gore speak at Stanford, along with an ad for Gore's new book. Recognizing that Buchheit must have worked all night to make his rogue dream come true, Mayer decided to let him sleep before chewing him out. But as Mayer stewed and Buchheit slumbered, her view began to change. The ads were actually useful. By the time Buchheit made it in to work, Google's founders Larry Page and Sergey Brin had also seen the ads and given the thumbs-up.

Gmail launched on April 1, 2004, to a limited group of a thousand invitees, with April Fool's Day chosen as a playful acknowledgment that the proposition of getting a free gigabyte of email seemed outrageous. One gigabyte was five hundred times the capacity offered by leading rival Hotmail. Many people did think the announcement was a joke. Many more, however, agreed with Mayer that the ads were just wrong. They found the description of how the service would be targeting them appalling. Pundits, politicians, and rights groups piled on criticism. By April 6, thirty-one organizations and advocates had signed a letter demanding Gmail be suspended. California state senator Liz Figueroa went so far as to tell Google that Gmail was a "disaster of enormous proportions, for yourself, and for all of your customers."

Once Gmail got into users' hands, however, they raved about it. Before long, invites to get a free Gmail account were selling on eBay for more than $150. Today, true to Buchheit's vision, Gmail has more than 1 billion happy users, and from a profitability standpoint, Buchheit's creepy invention has been a home run.

The pursuit of a better way sometimes requires us to disobey—to bend or break rules and offend the guardians of the status quo. Our bosses and organizations explicitly place some of these rules on us. To create Gmail, Buchheit had to contend with a rule so important in business as to be nearly universal—that one must follow direct orders from a superior. Then there are rules we've been taught and have internalized since childhood, the norms and morals of our culture. When Buchheit, a guy who cared deeply about ethics, was told his innovation was wrong, indecent, and even evil, he had to contend with his own internal pressure not to buckle and fold. Fortunately for Google and for more than a billion users, he pressed on.

A good deal of research agrees that being highly creative simply isn't compatible with always playing by the rules. Francesca Gino, a researcher at Harvard, explored this relationship when she invited people to take three tests in her lab. The first and third were creativity tests. The middle one, which participants were told they could make money on, was a simple matter of adding up numbers. Gino made it easy for test takers to cheat on the second test because they scored themselves and self-reported their performance based on an honor system. They didn't know that Gino's team could secretly spot and note their numerous transgressions.

The researchers found that those who cheated tended to be more creative than their noncheating peers. Perhaps this means creative people are more likely to cheat. In fact, Gino concluded as much: "Across all our studies . . . greater creativity promotes dishonesty by increasing individuals' ability to justify their unethical actions," Gino wrote with her colleague Dan Ariely.

But here was the more surprising result: participants' creativity scores improved on the last test, over the baseline they'd established on the first, if they cheated on the middle test. Gino concluded that because creativity so often requires bending the rules, getting a bit of practice at rule bending primes our brains to be more creative with the next thing we try.

Not only does being creative make us more likely to be dishonest, Gino would find, but being dishonest builds our creativity muscles.

Arizona State University's Zhen Zhang also found a consistent correlation between a tendency to break rules and creative success later in life. Among the white male subjects he studied, minor infractions committed in adolescence—like playing hooky and defacing property—predicted much higher chances of becoming a successful entrepreneur later in life.

Of course, indiscriminate and antisocial rule breaking can quickly become a drain on our internal resources. Break too many rules too often, and you have to spend valuable time and energy avoiding punishment, trying to repair broken relationships, and dealing with a troubled conscience. Writer Wallace Stegner summed up the balance we should strive for simply: "It is the beginning of wisdom when you recognize that the best you can do is choose which rules you want to live by. It's persistent and aggravated imbecility to pretend you can live without any."

Because we gain a boost of creativity when we bend or break rules, and because there's often much to find where others dare not go, we grow by actively looking for opportunities to do so. The problem is, of course, that we often pay a price for such defiance.

The Cost of Creativity

Classrooms, companies, and governments set rules for many good reasons, such as to increase predictability, minimize risk, and create harmony. In contrast, new, breakthrough ideas are usually unpredictable and risky and upset established patterns. That's why companies and managers so often talk about how much they value creativity, then reject it once they see it, forcing creative individuals to lie, cheat, and steal to bring their ideas to life.

Two researchers, Erik Westby and V. L. Dawson, wondered if this odd love-hate relationship was infecting our earliest experiences—that is, if teachers might be inadvertently giving the wrong signals to young children about the value of creative thinking. Ask teachers how they feel about creativity, and they'll quickly tell you it's a critical skill. One survey found that 96 percent think it's so important that daily class time should be devoted to teaching it. But do teachers actually like and value creative kids?

To find out, Westby and Dawson picked ten traits common to highly creative children and ten traits least typical of them. Creative traits included nonconformist, determined, individualistic, and progressive; not so creative traits: tolerant, practical, reliable, and dependable. Then each teacher was asked to rate a favorite and a least favorite student on all twenty traits. You can probably guess the direction this went but probably not the degree. All the teachers surveyed chose for their least favorite child kids whose traits marked them as highly creative. And all but one chose for their most favorite child a kid who was low on creativity. Even kids themselves, perhaps picking up signals from teachers, don't seem to think much of their creative classmates. Another study found that peers considered highly creative students the most ill behaved.

Being a teacher's least favorite student is a real disadvantage for a young person. Westby and Dawson concluded from their study that modern classrooms were starting young people out with the clear but inadvertent message that creativity just isn't desirable or acceptable.

Early in our lives, we start learning that originality can come at a cost. We do well to heed but not overlearn this lesson. To loosen the grip of fear that comes with rule breaking, we can make a habit of asking, "What problem does this rule exist to solve?" and then "Is there another, better way to try solve that problem?" This simple thought experiment can open up new possibilities, as long as it doesn't lead to the sort of cheating that induces shame and anxiety.

Buchheit knew that Google, like most workplaces, required employees to listen when their manager said to kill an idea because the company didn't want rogue products in the marketplace or employees wasting valuable time. So he found a way around these obstacles. He built AdSense overnight on his own time and launched it only among the handful of users who were running a pilot version of the tool. In this way he broke the rules but not the trust of his manager or his company. Certain times, however, call for far greater—and riskier—defiance.

◇◇◇◇◇◇◇

The year is 1983, and Barry Marshall's gut is on fire. It's time, he realizes reluctantly, to tell his wife, Adrienne, what he's done; why he's been jumping out of bed at 6:30 every morning, arriving at the toilet just in time for clear water to spew from his stomach; why she's noticed his breath fiercely stinking; why he can barely work.

Ten days before, Marshall sheepishly admits, he'd downed a glass of beef broth into which he'd stirred several billion *Helicobacter* organisms taken from the gut of one of his very sick patients. Adrienne's familiar with the bacterium; in fact her husband's been singularly focused on it for the last two years.

The obsession began in 1981, when Marshall, a third-year resident, was looking for a project to meet his licensing requirements. At the backwater hospital in western Australia where he was working, he met a pathologist named Robin Warren who gave the young doctor an intriguing starting point to work from. Warren said he'd noticed some unusual spiral-shaped organisms in all of his ulcer patients and wanted to understand why they were there.

Marshall, like everyone else at the time, knew that stress and habits like unhealthy eating and smoking caused stomach ulcers. A bad day at work, an annoying spouse, overeating for the fifth time that week—these were the kinds of things people would regularly complain were "giving me an ulcer." What, then, were these bacteria doing there?

For everyone who had them, ulcers were excruciating, and for some, they led to stomach cancer and death. At the time 2 to 4 percent of people in the Western world were being treated with antacids, though antacids were only a Band-Aid, not a cure. Those who couldn't muddle through with the drugs were visiting psychiatrists to reduce their stress or surgeons to cut out pieces of their digestive tract. Treating ulcers was a multi-billion-dollar industry that Barry Marshall was about to crash into headfirst.

Marshall remembers Warren giving him a list of twenty infected patients. A few days later one of them, an eighty-year-old Russian man, happened to limp into Marshall's office with severe intestinal pain. There wasn't much the inexperienced doctor thought he could do for the patient who was too old and frail for surgery, so, thinking about Warren's mysterious bacteria, he gave him antibiotics. "Two weeks later he comes back," Marshall recalls. "He's got a spring in his step, he's practically doing somersaults into the consulting room. He's healed. Clearing out the infection had cured him."

A strong feeling was now stirring in Marshall that perhaps everyone had it wrong. What if *Helicobacter* was causing ulcers? What if you could treat them with a course of antibiotics? So, like any good doctor he set out to follow the established path for testing his hypothesis. He arranged for a clinical study of one hundred patients and found the bacteria in 100 percent of those who had ulcers.

"When we submitted our research, it was rejected across the board," Marshall remembers.

Marshall says he tried to be patient. He understood that in the scientific process, it's the job of others in the field to shoot new ideas down and for the creator of those ideas to find the evidence to bring skeptics over to his or her side. But as one rejection rolled in after the next, he began to suspect that doctors who saw thirty ulcer patients a week, at $1,000 a visit, might never be interested in a very cheap onetime cure, even if it saved lives.

"It was desperate: I saw people who were almost dying from bleeding ulcers, and I knew all they needed was some antibiotics, but they weren't my patients," Marshall later told *Discover* magazine. "So, a patient would sit there bleeding away, taking the acid blockers, and the next morning the bed would be empty. I would ask, 'Where did he go?' He's in the surgical ward; he's had his stomach removed."

The obvious next step would have been for Marshall to run clinical trials of the treatment on enough people, and not just his own patients, to prove or disprove his theory. (He says you can't run these experiments on animals.) Without the support of the medical community, however, he would never be allowed to run such a trial. The rules were clear. You want to test a treatment on humans? You ask permission, then wait for approval. You can ask as many times as you like, but if permission doesn't come, you eventually give up.

Like so many rules designed to impose order and predictability, those Marshall had to contend with are double-edged. On the one hand, they save lives, even if they do slow down the process of bringing cures to market. On the other hand, the powerful can abuse them in their own interests. In this case, those with a vested interest in continuing to sell drugs and treatment were using them to circle the wagons, despite plenty of indications that Marshall and Warren were on the road to a discovery of enormous benefit.

Marshall wasn't willing to play by these rules, and so he'd taken the unconventional—many would say unethical—step of running a clinical trial of one with himself as the subject. That's how he'd come to drink the contaminated beef broth and why he'd gotten so sick.

"If you've ever done a parachute jump or bungee jump it's probably the feeling you have just before you leap off into space," Marshall told me of the moment he downed the concoction.

Marshall tells his wife that the experiment has worked. The bacteria have totally overrun his digestive system, and he now has gastritis, the first stage of ulcer formation. He's given himself an ulcer not through stress, smoking, or unhealthy food but through an infection. Marshall is elated, but Adrienne is terrified that he will infect the whole family. She insists that he end the experiment—now. He asks for a couple more days. She reluctantly agrees. That weekend he takes antibiotics and cures himself.

"It was a bit of luck that I got rid of it," Marshall admitted to me. "A friend of mine did it a year later and he had it for three years. I only took a single antibiotic."

As a result of his self-inflicted infection, the backwater Australian doctor finally begins to get noticed. Not by the *Lancet* or the *Journal of the American Medical Association*, as he had hoped, but by the *National Enquirer* and *Reader's Digest*, publications that get wind of his story and think the mad-scientist antics of the "guinea-pig doctor" who experimented on himself will delight readers. These stories give Marshall his first notice in the United States. Next, intrigued by the science as well as the character behind it, *New York Times* medical correspondent Lawrence Altman picks up on Marshall's work. "I've never seen the medical community more defensive or more critical of a story," Altman later recalled of the reaction to the positive piece he published. The tide, however, begins to turn. The Food and Drug Administration and National Institutes of Health finally look at the data and, after speaking with Marshall, decide to fast-track trials through the system. The results come back with irrefutable evidence that a simple course of antibiotics can, in most cases, treat ulcers.

By 1996, Marshall says, his screwball idea was becoming conventional wisdom. "If you're successful, the censure dies out pretty quickly." In 2005, Marshall and Warren received a Nobel Prize in medicine. Ulcers have gone from a lifelong scourge to a largely treatable nuisance, and stomach cancer has mostly disappeared from the developed world.

Disobeying Wisely

Marshall's description of his path to a cure paints a picture of a man willing to respect, seek to understand, and attempt to work within the rules but never to allow them to supersede his commitment to a much higher goal: ending the suffering of millions. That approach may sound simple, but Marshall's actions make him an almost unique outlier in the medical community. His refusal to take no for an answer and his wildly creative (albeit dangerous) response remain legendary among doctors and researchers thirty-five years later.

This attitude toward rules and rule breaking has a name: intelligent disobedience. Writer Ira Chaleff brought it to the business world's attention, inspired by his observations of how guide dogs are trained to behave at work. Imagine a blind woman and her trusted dog. For the duo to function, the dog must be instantly responsive to his owner and make her goals his own. What happens, though, when the owner tells the dog to step off the curb, but the dog sees a car coming that might kill one or both of them? Amazingly, without abstract thought or verbal language, guide dogs can be taught to disobey with the same commitment to a higher purpose that Marshall had. They will ignore a direct command that goes against the best interest of the team. Without that ability, neither owner nor dog would be remotely safe.

Intelligent disobedience is a compelling concept and easy to prescribe, but for every Paul Buchheit or Barry Marshall, there are many more Abtin Buergaris.

To pay his way through law school, Buergari took a job with a firm that did electronic discovery, the somewhat mind-numbing process of going through emails, instant messages, and digital documents to find information relevant to litigation. Although the material was all electronic, the search method used by the firm, and the wider industry, was strangely low-tech. Buergari had to read through the documents, one at a time.

Then a client came in with a rather simple request: please get through this giant pile of documents as quickly and cost-effectively as possible. The challenge had, Buergari realized, a simple solution. Get computers to scan the data looking for the same key words and phrases he was searching for with his slow and fallible human eyes. Excited about the time this could obviously save, Buergari brought the idea to his boss, who was strangely dismissive, hostile even. Surely, Buergari reasoned, he hadn't developed his idea enough to prove its merit, so he hammered out some of the details and brought it back to his boss again.

Again he was rejected. This time Buergari believed that because the average client spends $3 million per case for discovery, his firm didn't want the process to be faster and thus cheaper. The news was depressing, but still Buergari saw an opportunity. What if he built his tool on his own and became a contractor? He could bang out the discovery at lightning speeds and charge his employer much less than it was paying him to do it by hand, and the firm could go on charging its customers premium prices. Apparently, that suggestion didn't sit well with his managers. Buergari was promptly fired and then preemptively sued for trying to steal clients.

Fortunately for Buergari, and for anyone who has to pay for electronic discovery, he survived the attacks by his former employer and founded a business that would grow to two hundred employees in twelve offices around the world. Despite his success, his story, which will be familiar to anyone who's worked in a bureaucracy or large corporation, shows just how resistant work cultures can be to change and how punitive they can become when they sense dissent.

So how can we bring intelligent disobedience into our organizations without getting our heads chopped off? Research shows that it's a two-way street. As employees, we can cleverly increase our chances of getting away with rule breaking with a few critical strategies. And as leaders we can design our organizations to benefit from rather than punish positive rule-breaking behavior.

If you're looking to engage in a little intelligent disobedience, there is no guarantee you won't be punished. Buergari did just about everything right and still lost his job. Still, a large body of research on organizational dissent and rule breaking offers two approaches that are likely to cool the ire of gatekeepers and get a rule-breaking innovation through.

First, be open about dissatisfaction with creativity-killing rules. While pushing back on company policy can get us labeled as troublemakers, we're far more likely to make enemies by resisting in secret. Jeffrey Kassing, who's made a career of studying organizational dissent, says there are two types of resistors in an organization: those who speak out about their opposition, known as articulated dissenters, and those who act on it quietly, called latent dissenters. Colleagues and managers are more likely to see the quiet latent dissenter as disloyal and, surprisingly, as more verbally aggressive and argumentative. Articulated dissenters may wear their concerns on their sleeves, but they are more likely to be perceived as satisfied, influential, and committed and as having good relationships with their managers. So, perhaps counterintuitively, if we're going to break a rule, we're often better off doing it in the open rather than in secret.

Next, it's important to articulate the pro-social value of breaking a rule rather than the personal reason for doing so. Managers are more likely to forgive a violation committed in the interest of customers, coworkers, or society as a whole rather than to help an individual employee achieve a personally important goal or rectify a private grievance. Barry Marshall's action in finding a cure for ulcers, for instance, majorly violated medical norms, but his altruistic intentions and contributions were so obvious that he was quickly forgiven. Marshall never complained about not being noticed or allowed to do his work. He always couched his pursuit in terms of his passion to help millions of ulcer sufferers.

Encouraging Others to Rebel

Even when we rebel thoughtfully, we may still find ourselves punished by rigid, corrupt environments like the one Buergari toiled in. Ultimately, however, his firm lost out when his innovation changed the industry. As Ira Chaleff writes of intelligent disobedience, "Even those issuing the wrong orders will benefit from our having made the right choice." He's right, but only if leaders are thoughtful enough to create cultures that can accept a bit of defiance, that tolerate and even at times celebrate disobedience. It's hard to imagine Paul Buchheit having taken the chance he did in building Gmail if Google's culture regularly punished the smallest acts of defiance.

Just tolerating dissent, of course, is not enough. The "favorite student" study tells us that most people in our organizations have been raised in a culture that prizes compliance and punishes free-ranging independent thought. For intelligent disobedience to take hold, leaders, like guide dog trainers, must teach it.

Chaleff tells a vivid story of an army captain who replaced an extremely authoritarian predecessor. Not long after his arrival on base, the new captain approached one of his young lieutenants and issued a command, to which the lieutenant snapped to attention and said, "Yes, sir!" But the captain didn't leave it at that.

"Did that order I just gave you make sense?" he asked.

The lieutenant without thinking repeated, "Yes, sir!" though now he was starting to get nervous. In fact, the order was a test to see if the lieutenant could think for himself, which, thanks to his former commanding officer, he was not particularly equipped to do. When the captain asked a second time, the lieutenant stammered that he wasn't sure.

"Lieutenant, I cannot have you go off and execute something in my name if you are not clear what the order is or if, from your knowledge of the situation on the ground, you do not think it is a smart thing to do."

When the lieutenant replied again with a "Yes, sir!" the captain took him through a strange drill. He gave the young man orders and had him reply, "That's BS, sir!" until he was able to do it in a loud and firm voice.

For the next few weeks, the lieutenant practiced understanding his orders and questioning them when they didn't make sense. Then one day, the base's colonel called the captain and the lieutenant into his office. The colonel had a nephew also stationed on the base who had gotten into trouble. He asked the lieutenant if he could help get his nephew out of hot water. This time it wasn't a test.

"Sir, that's BS, sir," the lieutenant confidently replied. The colonel's eyes bulged out of his head, but before he could act, the captain stepped in.

"It's all right, sir, I'll take care of this," he said. Then he hustled the lieutenant out of the room.

"Well done," he said when the colonel was out of earshot. Then he went back in to appease their angry superior.

The captain in this story was doing a few critical things that all leaders who want to introduce productive rule breaking into their organizations should consider: he went out of his way to highlight the unacceptability of blind obedience, had his subordinate practice thoughtful but firm resistance, and then protected him when he employed it in a high-stakes situation. The captain was ensuring that he would get the benefit of the full intelligence and creativity of his subordinates when he needed it. That ultimately would give him far more power than controlling a unit of automatons.

If training our reports to be insubordinate feels like a bridge too far, Kassing has another solution. He says organizations can effectively encourage productive rule breaking simply by celebrating it when it's being done well. We can do this by looking for instances of "positive deviance." The concept comes from the world of public health, where researchers have discovered that in communities beset by challenges, you will often find some families that are relatively thriving. They're working with the same limited food sources, for example, but perhaps they're eating several small meals a day rather than one big one, or they're mixing in a traditional and widely available plant to supplement their nutrition. The idea has found its way into workplaces. In organizations that are stifling creativity with meetings, timesheets, and long chains of approvals, you'll often, if you look hard enough, find a rebel or two working around the system to be innovative and effective. Researchers say these are often low-status individuals in terms of hierarchy.

If we find these rebels, it's natural to celebrate their accomplishments while keeping their transgressions hushed up. But these deviants offer important lessons through their workarounds. Uncovering and sharing their stories indicates to everyone that intelligent disobedience is acceptable and can even be rewarded. Of course, we should also work to eliminate the unhelpful rules positive deviants had to flout in the first place.

Keeping Rules at Bay

It's possible that no organization has been more successful at harnessing the creativity of rule-flouting rebels without descending into utter chaos than Burning Man, the annual arts festival that has become a worldwide phenomenon. Each year more than 100,000 people flock to the desert, where they build a temporary city complete with multistory public buildings, transportation systems, schools, and hospitals. It's almost entirely self-organized by participants, yet disasters, like building collapses or violent crime, are rarer than in the outside world.

The festival's CEO, Marian Goodell, told me that unlike most companies, which tend to adopt hundreds of rules without much forethought simply because that's the way business is done, her leadership team spends a lot of time thinking about what few rules to allow into the organization and how many rules they can keep out.

"Making the event run more smoothly cannot be the only mission," she said after telling me that one of their rules was to minimize rules. "Having it be enjoyable, edgy, and not predictable—that has to be part of the decision-making process. Am I gonna close down all the avenues for mischief? That would be a huge mistake."

Goodell says the festival started out essentially lawless. Early participants brought guns and raced trucks across the desert, but over time, as the festival grew, organizers introduced minimal rules to protect safety and the spirit of the event.

"The whole goal is to set a landscape for others to experiment," she says. By not overplanning, Goodell has found that the community comes up with its own solutions to problems, people rely on each other's genius, and something rather unique emerges that has allowed Burning Man to completely redefine the festival experience without deteriorating into a free-for-all.

Not every organization has the luxury of starting life as an anarchist's dream of radical self-expression, but any organization can benefit from examining its rules, written and unwritten, to see which actually move teams toward their missions and which stifle creative action. While having a few rules that are meant to be broken can actually spur creativity, organizations should thoughtfully prune policies built up over time to address problems that may or may not still be relevant.

Breaking Our Own Rules

Even if we master resisting, skirting, and overcoming every bureaucratic restriction thrown our way, most of us are far from free to think as expansively and creatively as we'd like. Throughout our lives, conceptions of right and wrong have been drummed into us until a set of rules becomes embedded within our psyches. Conforming to them can become part of our identities. Once that happens, the limitations to our creativity come not from an overbearing teacher or shortsighted boss but from ourselves.

Any leadership or self-help book will tell you to cultivate a strong sense of values and a commitment to them. But this advice contains a real danger. If our values are to run our lives, we'd better examine them, expose ourselves to the values systems of others, and find ways to update our own. Our brains will resist this work, but if we don't do it, our creative possibilities will shrink as we grow more morally righteous. We become convinced that there's a right and wrong way to think and speak and that there are right and wrong people to listen to and work with. All of this inevitably makes us far less creative. This connection between moral rigidity and creative limitation makes intuitive sense, but a lot of research also supports it. For example, it is well known that the personality trait "openness to experience," which includes a readiness to reexamine social, political, or religious views, is strongly linked to creative performance. Dogmatism, on the other hand, is bad for one's creative health.

It's not easy, however, to maintain a truly open mind about morality. While we celebrate nearly any other type of flexibility, be it cognitive or physical, moral flexibility has an awful reputation. The words instantly bring to mind an ethics-for-sale approach to life. Why is that? It seems that this negative attitude toward revising one's moral positions may be hardwired into our brains.

In 2016, researchers from the University of Southern California (USC) recruited forty self-identified liberals to see what change in one key aspect of moral thinking, political belief, might look like in action. Each participant in the study was shown a statement and then a series of facts that might shake their belief in that statement. Not all facts were actually true, but they were rather persuasive. Some of the belief statements were political, like "Generally speaking, taxes on the wealthiest Americans should be increased." Others were not political at all, like "Lie detectors are generally unreliable." Not surprisingly, after viewing the "facts" that challenged their beliefs, participants said they had moved quite a bit on the apolitical statements but much less on the political ones. This makes sense. Why wouldn't we welcome some new, surprising info on lie detectors? And of course, we'll be hostile to attacks on deeply held moral beliefs. More interestingly, however, participants processed the information with entirely different parts of their brains, depending on whether the belief being challenged hit their moral sensibilities or not. Only challenges to political belief activated the structures of the brain that form the default mode network, which is involved in looking inward, disengaging from the external world, and constructing our sense of self. The researchers saw that challenges to our moral beliefs make us turn away from the outside world, perhaps to hide from troubling information and reassure ourselves that our identities are safe and secure. We're subconsciously reassuring ourselves that we need not change an important belief at the core of who we think we are.

One of the researchers, Jonas Kaplan, explained that updating your belief about who invented the light bulb doesn't change much about your life, but revising a core moral belief threatens to upend everything: "Changing values puts you against everyone around you," he said. "Is accepting this evidence worth it?"

So we're programmed at a neural level to resist examining and occasionally revising our values and morals. Earlier, I suggested that's exactly what we should try to do if we want to maintain creative flexibility. But is this a realistic goal? It can be, because there's a trick to unlocking, even just a little, the moral restrictions we put on ourselves. Learning that trick, as we'll see, starts with other people.

CHAPTER 11

Creating with the Enemy

Why we need friends who look like foes

T here's nothing overtly unusual about the suburban tea party taking place on a fall afternoon in 2013. A coffee table laid with homemade scones separates a middle-aged woman and two of her friends from a middle-aged man who's brought two friends of his own. The participants make friendly small talk. Upon closer look, it might seem strange that the hostess is wearing Lululemon yoga pants and a blue shirt layered over a purple one, while the host sports a large cowboy hat and large silver belt buckle. It's the only real clue so far that two very different cultures are colliding.

"Today we're going to talk about crony capitalism," says hostess Joan Blades, a cofounder of MoveOn.org, America's largest liberal activist community. MoveOn spends millions of dollars each election cycle supporting candidates on the left of the mainstream. In the 2016 presidential election, the community that Blades founded enthusiastically threw its considerable weight, and money, behind Vermont senator Bernie Sanders.

The cowboy has a mouth too full of scone to say much, but he nods, clearly approving of the topic and the baked good. Mark Meckler is a pro when it comes to tea parties. He's a founder of Tea Party Patriots, the organization behind the populist revolution that overran the Republican Party beginning in 2010, pushing it hard right.

The early part of the conversation unfolds as you might expect.

"Government hasn't done anything other than get in the way and deter people from getting things done," declares Linda Gilbert, a small-business owner who came to the get-together at Meckler's invitation.

"Did you go to public school?" responds Elisa Batista, one of Blades's friends. "Do the police patrol your streets?"

If not entirely helpful, the exchange is still far more civil than you might expect. Batista is speaking patiently and without strong emotion. Gilbert is listening.

Blades notes the back-and-forth with a smile.

"People are a lot harsher in impersonal circumstances," she told me later. "In person, they want to connect. They get it."

As the conversation continues, the group members begin to trust each other more and, to their surprise, to agree.

"They don't care about us. They don't care about poor kids," Meckler says of those doing favors in Washington for their big-money sponsors. "They don't care about small-business owners. They're just playing the politics of hate." Everyone nods, and even the liberals jump in to build off Meckler's comment.

The conversation becomes wide ranging—education, prison, the deficit. Before it ends, the participants have agreed on several key political issues, but more importantly they've made some of their first friends on the other end of the political spectrum. An op-ed written by Blades and Republican strategist Grover Norquist about prison reform would ultimately grow from this conversation. And this was only one of hundreds of "transpartisan" conversations that Blades's organization (aptly named Living Room Conversations) would spawn across the country and the world.

Blades said that Meckler is charming, warm, and fun to converse with. I imagined this would actually make the interaction even more threatening for Blades's moral brain. Who wants to get too close to a charismatic, intelligent agent of the other side? Isn't that experience even more threatening to our stable identities than facts flashed on a screen?

Blades says the setup of Living Room Conversations avoids this cognitive resistance. "We invite people not to come too convince, but to listen," Blades explains. "It's not about changing people's minds as much as making human connections, opening their hearts. And it's about making us all smarter and more creative in the solutions we can come up with."

Blades says in her own Living Room Conversations, she hasn't done much to move her conservative friends over to her side. Instead, they've come to understand her much better, and now they sometimes find themselves caring about issues they wouldn't otherwise, like the environment, because they care about their friend Joan. The care, says Blades, runs both ways.

"Listening to people who are different than you is like a puzzle or a math problem that's not easy to solve. It's not easy but it stretches your brain. And we need that, because if we want to solve our big problems, our wicked problems, we need everyone's best ideas in the room and the flexibility to learn and improve our fixes together."

Meckler and Blades have intuitively hit upon a brain hack whose value science is now confirming. While it was easy, in fact largely automatic, for the liberal study participants to immunize themselves against unwelcome ideas when they saw them on a computer monitor in the USC study, actually connecting human to human over an extended period with people, not just ideas, from the other side gives us all a creative problem-solving boost. In a surprising and widely quoted experiment, the University of Michigan's Scott E. Page and Lu Hong of Loyola University showed that groups selected at random tend to be more effective at solving complex problems in fields like business, public policy, and education than even handpicked groups of the best and brightest experts.

"This is because the random group is more likely to contain a diversity of approaches to these tasks," explains Page. The experts are all likely to follow similar strategies and duplicate each other's work. But the random group, because its members have different perspectives and ideologies, Page says, will more quickly overcome any shared weaknesses.

"The problems we face in the world are very complicated. Any one of us can get stuck," he explains. "If we're in an organization where everyone thinks in the same way, everyone will get stuck in the same place. But if we have people with diverse tools, they'll get stuck in different places. One person can do their best, and then someone else can come in and improve on it."

These findings should throw up warning signals for the growing number of organizations proudly declaring that they hire for cultural fit over skills (Google calls their cultural fit Googliness). Without a doubt, we want to keep negative, destructive personalities off our teams, but how quickly can culture fit come to mean people who think like we do, care about what we care about, and employ the same mind-sets we do? Blades says many of her progressive friends are totally comfortable believing that Donald Trump voters are all racist. Who would want to work with a racist? There's certainly no "culture fit" there. But in shunning and excluding those they think of as different or dangerous, these liberals (and conservatives are no better) are depriving themselves of opportunities to expand their creativity. It was just such an opportunity that allowed a reverend named Jeffrey Brown to help bring down murders by 79 percent in a neighborhood that was spiraling toward out-of-control violence.

Seeking Out the Unlikeliest Allies

Brown began his ministry at the Union Baptist Church in Cambridge, Massachusetts, as a young man with dreams of building an empire. He envisioned turning the modest congregation into a 15,000-seat megachurch. He wanted his own TV channel and to build a ubiquitous brand that would spread the word of God, and his face, around the nation. Those dreams, he quickly realized, would have to wait. The community he had stepped into was experiencing an outbreak of violence that was weekly leaving young people shot dead in the streets, in the playgrounds, and just outside the doors of the church Brown hoped to take into the stratosphere.

"At that point in the 1990s people had stopped talking about solving the violence problem," Brown told me. "They said we had to cope with it because violence was here to stay." That accepting attitude seemed insane and immoral to a man who regularly had to preach over the sound of gunshots.

Brown became increasingly infuriated by the senseless killing, and as he ministered to the distraught family members of shooting victims, his thoughts of national stardom turned to a calling much closer to home. His first plan to cure the violence epidemic was simple: He would find the good kids who were at risk of falling in with the wrong crowd. He would catch those on the fence before they got sucked in, and eventually killed, by the gangbangers and drug dealers who seemed to think nothing of shooting someone for a few dollars or just to earn a harder reputation. Brown tried to get these at-risk youth to come to church, to gain protection and redirection, but few showed up, and week by week the killings continued.

Then one night in 1990, a young man named Jesse McKie was walking home with a friend when two neighborhood youths approached. They leveled guns at McKie and demanded his jacket. When he turned it over, one of them decided to pull the trigger anyway. McKie staggered along the sidewalk, looking for help. He died a hundred yards from Brown's church.

"But even if he had made it to the church, it wouldn't have mattered," Brown says. "It was nighttime, and nobody was home."

Brown took McKie's death hard and saw it as a message that for all of his passionate preaching, he and his church were irrelevant in the fight to save young people from the menace that awaited them after dark on the streets. As he pondered this, Brown realized he actually had no idea what his streets looked like during the killing hours.

"There were shootings every night," he recalls. "Stepping out there was harrowing, but in my heart I knew I had to do it." So Brown recruited a few other ministers, and they began to walk, heading out at 10 p.m. each night, often not returning until 3 a.m. In those dark parking lots and playgrounds, Brown didn't find the good kids at risk of falling in with the bad guys. Instead he found the dealers and the shooters themselves, and he says they were nothing like the cold and heartless monsters he had assumed they would be.

"There was this group of youth who used to sell drugs in a park. The park was surrounded by a chain link fence, and at the door to the fence there was a guy whose job it was to decide who got in and out. He's one of the guys who carried a gun, an enforcer, and he never said a word to us." Then one night, the young man stepped forward, grabbed one of Brown's colleagues, and took him around the corner while the rest waited in stunned fear for their friend to return.

"Bob comes back, and we all grabbed him. 'What did he say?' The young man told Bob that he had a question. He said that with all he'd done he'd seemed to have lost his conscience. He wanted to know if he could get his conscience back."

Through encounters like this, Brown's moralistic worldview began to crumble. He found the kids he met, who were the very sources of the violence, were themselves scared to be on the streets. They were trapped in a situation they didn't know how to get out of. And while they liked gold chains and ostentatious rings, Brown realized, they were no more materialistic than his friends who ran off to the mall each weekend to shop for sport. Had someone tried to simply convince him of these ideas, his brain would have filtered out the arguments as threats to his core belief system. But standing face-to-face with these youth at 2 a.m. shut that resistance down.

"I never thought I'd have a faith conversation with a drug dealer," Brown told me. "But on the streets, with these youth, I had some of the most profound conversations of my life."

In a widely shared TED talk, Brown recounts the realization that these first contacts on the streets created.

> In all of those sermons that I preached decrying the violence, I was also talking about building community, but I suddenly realized that there was a certain segment of the population that I was not including in my definition of community. And so the paradox was this: If I really wanted the community that I was preaching for, I needed to reach out and embrace this group that I had cut out of my definition. Which meant not [just] building programs to catch those who were on the fences of violence, but to reach out and to embrace those who were committing the acts of violence.

This is not, however, just a feel-good story about one man's widening respect for a diverse humanity. This was a key moment in the genesis of what criminologists and sociologists would come to call the Boston Miracle, the beginning of one of the most successful violence-prevention campaigns in modern American history, which would bring murder rates down by more than 70 percent in Brown's neighborhood and create precipitous drops in other cities across America.

Maybe it was fear of how these hardened youths might respond if he started preaching to them. Maybe it was a bit of guilt about how he had stereotyped them in the past. For whatever reason, as Brown walked the streets, he felt a strong urge not to tell these kids what to do but instead to listen. What did *they* think was needed to bring down the violence?

"The answers they gave me were surprising," Brown recalls. Right away the gang members pointed out the problem of school vacations. They told him these were out-of-control times because they had no-where to go and nothing to do. Sure enough, Brown found there were major murder spikes during breaks. The police knew this of course, but they hadn't found a solution to the predictable problem. "The young people said we need a place to hang and what about the school gym? I spoke to the principal about the idea and he was kind of shocked. But we made the arrangements to open up the basketball court, get a bad-minton court going, give them a PA system to play music on. The first night 1,100 youth showed up. There was no trouble." Crime dropped to a trickle that week. The kids, like kids anywhere, simply needed a place to have fun and redirect their energy. It gave them something to do other than fight and kill.

Some of the gang members asked Brown to connect them to micro-finance loans so they could start legitimate small businesses. "Once you take a drug dealer out of the drug business, you have a young entrepreneur," he contends. Several of the youth launched successful ventures and began to employ their friends.

"We stopped looking at them as a problem to be solved and we started looking at them as partners, as assets and collaborators," Brown says. "You have a minister at one table and a heroin dealer at the other table, coming up with a way in which the church can help the entire community. Alone we couldn't see the solutions, but together we could."

Brown's work developed into a policing program known as Operation Ceasefire, in which Brown remained influential. Ceasefire called for the community, including police, clergy, and community activists, to identify young people most engaged in violence and call them in for a face-to-face meeting. Two messages would be issued: the next group to shoot someone would face an immediate crackdown, but those who wanted to turn their lives around would get help and a seat at the table to develop solutions for their own communities. Operation Ceasefire brought gun murders in Stockton, California, down by 42 percent. Indianapolis saw a 34 percent drop. From 1990 to 1999, annual homicides in Boston dropped from 152 to 31.

I asked Brown about his own journey to put aside his anger and disdain for the violent youth who had been terrorizing his community and standing in the way of his own dreams of fame. Surely nobody is more adept at praising good and condemning evil than an aspiring televangelist. Wasn't it difficult to set aside his indignation and judgment to work with these young people? Brown said it would have been impossible had he not gone out and met them face-to-face. Like with Joan Blades's Living Room Conversations, the simple act of sitting down to listen to the perceived enemy opened up creative avenues and solutions that would have remained invisible to a group with a strongly shared set of values and perspectives.

Ingenious and lifesaving as Operation Ceasefire proved, it lost steam in the next decade because it's just not natural for people to wrap their minds around solutions that defy narrow moral categories. In city after city, once the champions of the program in the police force moved on, a new regime would come in and drift away from Ceasefire's core principles.

"It has no natural constituency," Thomas Abt, a Harvard Kennedy School researcher, told *ProPublica*. "To vastly oversimplify, progressives want more prevention and conservatives want more enforcement." An approach that refuses to tolerate violent behavior but also refuses to demonize violent offenders, Abt says, "challenges the orthodoxy on both sides. It makes everybody uncomfortable."

This discomfort is natural in a world of rigid conceptions of right and wrong. When it sweeps ingenious ideas off the table, however, that discomfort becomes tragic. Rules, firm values, and moral systems hold our world together and restrain people's worst impulses. But they also constrain and limit our creativity, and thus we should treat them with far more skepticism than we usually do.

The persistence of right-versus-wrong thinking is an inevitable part of the difficult road unsafe ideas face when they leave the minds of innovators and reach wider groups of people, because groups, as we will see, are naturally rule enforcing, moralistic, and safety seeking. For unsafe ideas to thrive, we must learn to infect others around us with a willingness to think and behave with more flexibility and boldness. We turn to how to do that next.

MORALITY: KEY TAKEAWAYS

Practice disobedience . . .

Obey all the time, and you'll vastly limit your creativity. Disobey without forethought, and you'll likely be cast off your team or out of your organization. Ira Chaleff uses guide dogs as a model of "intelligent disobedience," and it's a good one—be absolutely committed to the cause but never take orders blindly.

When you encounter rules that limit your creativity, first suggest they be changed, and if that doesn't work, be open about your intention to break them. Others will appreciate you for it. Design your rebellion to maximize the benefit to others, and you're most likely to be forgiven.

. . . And teach disobedience to others

We all say we want more creativity, but our schools, our companies, and even our individual brains are set up to reward sheep-like behavior and punish those who chart their own paths. It's time to fight back.

What rules can your organization do without? Remember that minimizing unhelpful rules can release creativity. Do you take time to role-play dissent or tell stories about people who stepped out of bounds but benefitted their teams? Such storytelling tells people not only that dissent is acceptable but how to do it effectively.

Find unlikely allies

Most of us naturally resist sitting down with others who disagree with us. It threatens our identities and can feel like a betrayal of our tribes. But we can quickly grow our cognitive abilities and find hidden solutions in these unlikely relationships, as Jeffrey Brown did in his Boston neighborhood.

Do you take time to talk (and more importantly listen) to those on the other side? You may find that your perceived enemies can actually be your most productive allies.

PART 6

LEADERSHIP

CHAPTER 12

Unsafety in Numbers

How to break consensus and infect others
with the confidence to take risks

I n October 2014, Walgreens, America's largest retail drug store chain, issued a public statement. "We believe that if the goal is to truly reduce tobacco use in America, then the most effective thing retail pharmacies can do is address the root causes and help smokers quit," the company announced. "Our goal is to help get the U.S. smoking rate, which has leveled off at around 18% of the adult population for a decade, moving lower again."

Though this may sound like the kickoff for a big, bold antismoking campaign, it wasn't. Instead it was the company's rationale for continuing to sell millions of packs of cigarettes a year at the front of its stores. Hypocritical as the idea of a health and wellness company peddling tobacco while claiming to fight tobacco use might seem, the decision was hardly surprising. If it stopped selling cigarettes, Walgreens would have to give up more than $1 billion in annual revenue. And even if it took such bold action, Walgreens executives reasoned quite logically, customers could easily just go elsewhere to feed their addiction. In fact, the very idea of ending tobacco sales would have been inconceivable, except a few days earlier rival CVS, the second-largest retail drug store chain in the United States, had announced it would do just that.

"We had started internally two years before that decision creating a very common language around our culture and purpose," remembers

Helena Foulkes, the woman who championed the controversial decision through the behemoth organization. "Our purpose we defined as helping people on a path to better health." Though the purpose statement sounded straightforward and hard to argue with, it quickly started causing problems internally.

Whenever Foulkes, then chief of strategy and government affairs, spoke to her employees, some brave soul would inevitably ask, "If that's what we're about, then why are we selling cigarettes?" Foulkes says that question made her more and more uncomfortable. She wasn't alone. Nearly everyone in the company saw the irony of the situation. There was just a general, unspoken consensus that this was how things had always been and probably always would be.

Perhaps Foulkes was different because, for her, the discomfort wasn't only professional; it was personal. Foulkes is a cancer survivor, and five years earlier, her mother had died of lung cancer, the very disease her company was now putting millions of customers at risk of developing.

Had she just advocated from a position of personal discomfort, of course, Foulkes knew she would have gotten nowhere with the phasing out of tobacco across CVS's 7,800 stores. The chain was taking in about $2 billion a year from tobacco alone. Large internal business units, staffed by her friends and colleagues, depended on selling more. To redirect the organization, Foulkes and a team of coconspirators knew they'd have to craft a compelling case for the move.

Here's what Foulkes's revolutionaries argued: The United States was going through major shifts in health-care delivery, and CVS had already begun aggressive moves to take advantage of new markets created by the Affordable Care Act. They were in the process of expanding walk-in health clinics to treat patients on-site. At the same time, internal strategists were anticipating that rising deductibles would lead customers to shop around quite a bit more as they shelled out more cash for their drugs. All of this, Foulkes and her allies reasoned, would mean CVS's live-or-die growth opportunity would lie on the health-care side of the business. Retail items like cleaning supplies, candy, and tobacco would increasingly become a sideshow. Wouldn't it be insane to allow that sideshow to detract from the company's competitiveness in the booming health-care market? End cigarette sales, Foulkes advocated, and we'll more than make up for the losses with the partnerships and customers we attract as a true health company.

Described step-by-step and from a bit of a distance, Foulkes's case seems logical, perhaps even difficult to argue with. But anyone who's worked in an established organization knows just how often sound ideas that threaten short-term profits and everyday behavior can get plowed under. Walgreens had all the information Foulkes's team possessed but still found reasons to deny the logic, even after its main competitor took action. As we'll see in a moment, those reasons were deeply flawed, though that still hasn't changed the Walgreens strategy.

Foulkes says she spent more than a year advocating for the plan, slowly building momentum toward a commitment. Her work involved endless conversations aimed at breaking a consensus that selling cigarettes was just part of running a drugstore. No one thought to question it, beyond feeling privately discomfited, but she strongly believed this consensus was no longer serving the company. Foulkes worked carefully, using the moral argument with those she believed would follow their hearts and relying more heavily on the business case with those she felt would follow their heads. Little by little, her growing alliance gained the endorsement of the company's senior leadership.

Then, just before CVS finally announced it would end tobacco sales, Foulkes was thrust into a new position that would force her to face directly the effects of her evangelism. She was promoted to head up retail.

"I remember someone saying, 'so now do you think it's a good idea?'" Foulkes told *Fortune* magazine. She says she stuck to her belief but braced herself for panic as billions in sales disappeared off her books.

Within a week of launch, lifted by a flood of positive press, CVS's stock price was up, and it has continued a steady march in that direction since. A year after the decision, though front-of-store sales were down 8 percent, pharmacy benefit services were up 12 percent, and the company had signed $11 billion in new contracts made possible, it says, by its vastly improved reputation. And contrary to Walgreens' feeble prognostications, smoking is actually down in communities where CVS is present. According to one analysis of market retail data, 95 million fewer packs were purchased, at all retail locations, in the first year in these communities.

Foulkes and her allies' success in moving an enormous and bureau-cratic organization in a direction it had billions of reasons not to head is the exception rather than the rule. All too often, those with outlying ideas and a passion to promote them get roughly pushed to the side or patronized and ignored. Foulkes's story prompted me to ask, after more than a year of studying unsafe thinking in individuals, what it takes to get a group of people not only to entertain but to embrace and cham-pion unsafe ideas. The question is critical because change is not a solo endeavor. To have an impact on our organizations, communities, and fields, we need resources, creativity, and evangelism that we can only get from other people. Helena Foulkes's genius didn't spring from some outlying realization that a pharmacy shouldn't sell cigarettes or that the business model of pharmacies was changing. Everyone could see that. Instead her genius lay in her ability to lead a large, conservative organi-zation to take a highly unsafe leap.

Sure, there is the myth of the lone innovator, the brash rebel with the devil-may-care attitude who changes the world on his or her own. But in an exhaustive and widely accepted review of key innovators in art, science, and politics since ancient times, sociologist Randall Col-lins identified only three who truly acted alone (Confucian metaphys-icist Wang Ch'ung, fourteenth-century Zen master Bassui Tokusho, and fourteenth-century philosopher Ibn Khaldun). The rest, from Beethoven to Adam Smith to Charles Darwin to James Jamerson, the little-known cowriter of more number one hits than Elvis, the Beat-les, the Rolling Stones, and the Beach Boys combined, did their work from within a network of peers who shared, critiqued, and honed each other's ideas.

While we need other people, they are often deadly. The mere pres-ence of other people has been consistently shown to depress creativity, while groups tend to enforce all the attitudes of safe thinking we've been exploring ways to overcome: they rush too quickly to consensus, rally around expert leaders, punish dissenters, quickly harden their shared sense of right and wrong, and unless directed otherwise, squash risky and unfamiliar ideas in the name of efficiency and practicality.

Trying to practice unsafe thinking with others can lead in one of two directions. Either we will find ourselves frustrated and eventually silenced or ostracized from the group, or things can, as Helena Foulkes found, turn out for the better. Whether we sit atop an organization or find ourselves simply part of the team, we have the opportunity to infect an entire group with creativity and boldness. I ultimately discovered a well-tested set of practices to help us get to this outcome, and thus what began in this book as an individual journey of self-change now becomes one of cultivating leadership and a commitment to the growth of others.

In these final chapters, we'll look at two seemingly contradictory forces leaders at any level can apply to vastly increase the creativity and flexibility of those around them. One is disruption, and the other is security.

Through the force of disruption, we break the limiting consensus that often comes before a group has fully understood a situation. Like Foulkes, we push our teams to look at hard truths and engage in productive conflict, uncomfortable as this might seem. Disruption, of course, is psychologically taxing and threatening. People can only take so much of it before they burn out and shut down. That's why the counterforce of security becomes so necessary. As leaders, we become more successful when we make our team members feel as safe as possible in embracing unsafety. Those who know they are ultimately valued and protected, who are incentivized to take chances and aren't punished for mistakes, can embrace discomfort without having anxiety flood out their ability to create. We now turn to these counterforces, this yin and yang of group creativity.

Countering Conformity

Before Stanley Milgram ran his now legendary obedience experiment, he polled a group of forty psychologists. What percentage of ordinary men, he asked, do you expect will administer a near-deadly shock to an innocent victim just because an authority figure tells him to do so? They predicted, Milgram recollects, that little more than 1 in 1,000 participants would willingly stick with such a directive up to the highest level of punishment.

When Milgram had finished his experiment, however, a far less optimistic view of humanity emerged. Two-thirds of his participants followed orders to deliver what they believed was a 450-volt shock to an actor who pretended to writhe in pain and scream for mercy.

Milgram gave two explanations for these terrifying results. The first is the tendency toward conformity. Especially when the stakes are high, people quickly discount their own judgment when they feel it runs counter to the will of a group. Though we may see clearly that the course being pursued is insane, we tend to question our own sanity rather than resist the judgment of those around, and especially above, us. The second explanation is a tendency to obey. When others in a group are more powerful than us, we let go of our sense of responsibility for our actions. We rationalize that we're just following orders, which, while uncomfortable, is less frightening than resisting.

This is perhaps the best-known psychological experiment of all time. Less familiar is the follow-up work Milgram undertook to see what might interrupt such behavior. In what he called "Experiment 17," Milgram added two more actors to the situation who posed as people working alongside the participants. Now three people were in the room and being asked to administer the shocks. This changed everything. When the actors refused to comply, the participants woke up to the horror of the situation, and instead of following the ridiculous orders, they too took their hands off the controls. Under these conditions, only 10 percent went ahead and administered the shock.

Experiment 17 shows the enormous potential of individuals, through courageous action, to break the spell of conformity. It didn't take much. The actors didn't have to persuade the participant or point out the folly of continuing. They simply had to speak up, and the participant's willingness evaporated. These actors were like Foulkes, turning the inner whisperings of discomfort into clear commitment to a better way. And like Foulkes, these actors weren't even the appointed leaders in the situation. The powerful "experimenter," with his lab coat and clipboard, forcefully demanded that the experiment continue, but on seeing an act of disruption, 90 percent of people simply wouldn't keep going.

Official leaders, of course, have even more power to disrupt inappropriate consensus. Alfred P. Sloan Jr., GM's president in the 1920s, is said to have ended a meeting this way: "Gentlemen, I take it we are all in complete agreement on the subject here." His executives all nodded their heads, eager to move on to the next order of business. "Then, I propose we postpone further discussion of this matter until our next meeting, to give ourselves time to develop disagreement and perhaps gain some understanding of what the decision is all about."

Stanley Milgram, Helena Foulkes, and Alfred P. Sloan Jr. make it look easy to redirect groups of people heading in the wrong direction. In most cases, it's not. When Harvard's Francesca Gino asked 1,000 people if they worked in companies that encourage nonconformity, 900 said no. Speaking up for disruptive ideas is simply not encouraged, and it's not taught—in fact it's more often punished. Applying disruption without getting labeled a pain in the ass and an impediment to progress takes some subtle strategic action and an understanding of what makes seemingly good groups go bad.

Escaping the Trap of Agreement

Of the "Big Five" traits psychologists commonly use to describe an individual's personality, none is quite so appealing as "agreeable." Here are but a few of the lovely characteristics of highly agreeable people: they are trusting, easy to get along with, cooperative, sympathetic, and selfless. It's no wonder that high schoolers tend to rate their agreeable peers as more likable, while bosses prize their most agreeable employees as team players. When a bunch of agreeable people get together, however, they often wind up focusing more on making each other feel good than accomplishing anything of value.

Over a twenty-month period, the University of Richmond's Dejun Tony Kong watched forty-two teams take on a difficult change-management consulting project. He found that the teams made of highly agreeable people not only performed worse than more cantankerous teams but often couldn't tell when things were going wrong. They judged their satisfaction with their team based on how good it felt to be together rather than what they were getting done. Teams with a few disagreeable individuals showed a different pattern. Not only did they perform better, but their satisfaction tended to track well with their results. Feeling good came not from getting along but from making progress, and so they had a functional internal compass to guide them to success.

The first takeaway here is that we should stop spending so much energy trying to make others feel good, and if nobody else is doing it well, we should strive to be an occasionally disagreeable member of any group we're in. But Kong's study also highlights another important and subtle rule about teams: success derives from disagreement but not of the sort that depresses a team's satisfaction in working together. Perhaps the most disagreeable person I ever met once sauntered into a board meeting of a human rights organization halfway through the proceedings. He demanded we stop what we were doing and fill him in on the work so far. When we did, he puffed himself up and began to say things like "Well, I'm not part of your do-gooder world, but in the corporate world we take a much more rigorous approach." He challenged everything we had worked hard to construct and questioned our individual qualifications. Before long, I became aware he was trying to do something that made sense. He was trying to introduce a bit of grit to the proceedings, to break us out of our consensus. His efforts, however, were a disaster. Group satisfaction plummeted. The chair quietly asked him to stay away from the next day's meeting, and we went, as a group, right back to what we were doing before this self-styled gadfly walked into our lives.

Crafting Productive Conflict

We need not denigrate, embarrass, or resist our teammates to break out of the trap of agreeableness. Even kind and compassionate individuals can lower group agreeableness; in fact, they're likely better at doing so while keeping group satisfaction high. So how can we disrupt harmony without destroying morale? One way is to gamify disagreement by finding mechanisms that both encourage and depersonalize controversy. Here are some examples of how it's done.

On their show *Freakonomics Radio*, Steven Levitt and Stephen Dubner tell the story of a retail company set to open its first ever store in China. Two months before the opening, the CEO invites the leaders of the seven teams responsible for the effort into his office. He wants to know whether each leader's work is on track to open the store on time. Just pick one of three signals, the CEO asks, red, yellow, or green. Dubner and Levitt note that this company prizes agreeable people. Anyone who speaks negatively about the firm or its future is considered a naysayer or uncommitted. So, of course, each team leader says "green," and the meeting ends.

A few people have noticed that predictions around the company often fail, so they try a different approach to gauging the likelihood of the store's opening on time. They set up an internal prediction market. Everyone gets a little money to spend on "shares" of the prediction that the store will open on time. If that happens, the shares pay out real cash. If it doesn't, the value of the shares goes to zero. People are free to buy or sell these shares anonymously at any price they agree upon. It's just a game. It's fun, and it's also safe to express your true analysis of the situation without hurting anyone's feelings or getting in trouble.

According to the market, the store had only an 8 percent chance of opening on time. In fact, the deadline came and went, and the store wasn't even close to ready, despite every team leader's offering assurances that the project was on schedule. Dubner believes that the CEO had "go fever," a term used to describe a dangerous determination to plow ahead without getting the full picture of a situation. In the face of a go-fever-crazed CEO, it's hard for anyone to offer the truth or even recognize reality. But in the context of a game, the truth quickly emerges. Ford Motors, which regularly uses prediction markets, finds that they tend to perform 25 percent better than expert forecasts and that those who trade in these markets actually learn to become better predictors. It's surprisingly easy to set up an internal prediction market for any team situation through several free online services.

A lower-tech solution for gamifying disagreement is the use of red teams. The term comes from military war games in which the blue team represents our side and the military strategies we are considering using in the real world. The red team takes the role of the enemy, and its job, of course, is not to make the blue team feel good about itself. Red team members are supposed to expose every possible flaw in their opponents' plans and defeat them if possible. Despite the fierce competition, everyone playing the game knows they're actually on the same side with a common goal of making the chosen strategy better, and there's a culture of respect for those who run excellent red teams even though they occasionally best their colleagues or superiors.

This kind of approach can work for any group. As an idea gains traction and support, we can take a timeout and assign it a red team tasked with looking it over and raising every relevant objection or scenario in which it might fail. Objections like "You always come up with impractical ideas" are of course out of bounds. It's about the work product, not the producers. Objections should never be sugarcoated; no need to say "Well, I like the idea but . . ." On the other hand, challenges should always be delivered with respect to make sure teammates don't spike emotionally and cease hearing us. After carefully listening to the red team, an idea's proponents then step away and focus on addressing the objections they believe to be most important. Challenging as this exercise can be, red team games are often one of the most intellectually engaging and growth-oriented parts of a creative process. They crack agreeableness without cracking team bonds.

Gleaning Ideas from the Edges

Helena Foulkes's successful campaign to end tobacco sales had two key components. The first was challenging the consensus that pharmacy cigarette sales were inevitable and acceptable. She did this primarily by pointing out the insane disconnect between that practice and CVS's widely embraced purpose statement. It took an important second component, however, to push her plan to success. She had to bring attention to a set of new data on the periphery of the company's focus about the changing field of health care. This data ultimately turned the tide. But first she had to overcome a quirk of group psychology known as shared information bias, which can be even deadlier for unsafe ideas than too much agreeableness.

Imagine this scenario: Five people walk into a meeting to discuss an important strategic decision for the company. *Should we continue to sell tobacco in our pharmacies?* Now, let's say for simplicity's sake that the team members hold ten truly relevant pieces of information in aggregate. Everyone knows eight of those pieces. They've been widely discussed at the company and drummed by the CEO into everyone's heads. We're talking about clear, seemingly logical, accepted information. *Cigarette sales bring in $2 billion a year. Our customers will go elsewhere to buy tobacco if we cut off their supply. We can help our customers quit instead of giving up this line of business altogether.* But two pieces of information are held by only one team member each. This information, like that Helena Foulkes used to build her case, may contradict or at least add nuance to the group's conventional wisdom.

So what's the point of getting these five people together in a room? To make sure that all ten people have all ten pieces of information, so that they make the best decision, right? And we'd expect the people with the unique information to emerge as heroic bearers of important news. Actually, that's exactly the opposite of what usually happens. Shared information bias consistently and unconsciously drives groups to focus on the information everyone already has. People tend to feel safe discussing the obvious and for good reason; their colleagues are more likely to rate them as capable when they spout widely shared information, and group leaders favor obvious information more often. In fact, some studies have shown that the more power people have, the more they unintentionally inhibit the sharing of information from the edges, even shielding themselves from it. And low-status group members are most likely to be aware of the unique information the rest of the team can't see. This is partly because high-status members tend to communicate more broadly and often, so everyone already shares the information leaders possess. On the other hand, low-status individuals usually just keep quiet. If you've ever had the sense that a lot of meetings are a waste of time, shared information bias is one key reason you've probably been right.

If we want our teams to think differently, we need to gather ideas from the edges, and researchers have found a few ways to make sure this happens. High-status individuals should avoid sharing their thinking first. They rarely have the important outlying information, and by setting the tone, they further marginalize those who do. If you're a leader, I know, changing this habit can be hard. But here's a powerful trick suggested by those who study shared information bias: Take the time you would have used at the beginning of a meeting to express your views to instead discuss the importance of getting ideas from the edges. Indicate your desire to hear what the group doesn't already know. Then ask team members to jot down the important information they have before everyone starts talking. Any outlying information written down is much more likely to surface along the way. When we're not group leaders, we can remind ourselves that our team most needs the nonobvious information we hold and that withholding, tempting as it may be, is a disservice to our shared mission.

It's also been shown that team members who are part of minority groups are more likely to stay silent. We can work together to encourage each other to speak, recognizing that cultural bias is likely keeping some of us quiet. Finally, and this is perhaps the most unexpected finding I uncovered, important meetings should be *longer* when possible. Peripheral information often takes more time to emerge, and when we prize speed and efficiency, meetings can end before the ideas from the edges surface.

When productive conflict flourishes and information from the edges breaks through, risk taking and original ideas emerge, and the entire culture of an organization can begin to shift. While Foulkes, who's been promoted to CVS president in the years since her tobacco work, has spoken widely about the impacts of her internal campaign on public health, she is emphatic that the experience deeply changed the company as well. "[It's] been a catalyst both internally and externally for getting our organization to think differently, to think more boldly," she says. "People in the organization said wow that was a big bet. I can make big bets in my business." In 2017, CVS became the first pharmacy chain to remove candy from the front of its stores, a next and obvious step toward fulfilling the company's purpose.

Foulkes's claim that her disruption opened space for the company to embrace risk taking and bold thinking seems credible to me, though perhaps simplified. Leading by example alone isn't enough to keep groups out on the edge, and a constant culture of disruption can become exhausting. It takes a balancing force, a commitment to making team members feel safe, to keep unsafe thinking consistently flowing through a culture. To understand how that's done, I turned to a leader who's reached the top of his field by creating a culture of safety in an enormously competitive environment.

Making It Safe to Get Unsafe

Steve Kerr was the kind of player fans called unselfish. Though for some time the most accurate three-point shooter in the league, Kerr seemed content to dish to Michael Jordan or Scottie Pippen when the game was on the line.

Fans couldn't see, partly because his teammates were so damned good at making the shots Kerr set them up for, that Kerr wasn't unselfish. He was afraid of missing.

"I knew I wasn't good enough to afford to make many mistakes," Kerr told me, recalling the early days of his career, when many considered him less than NBA material. "So I passed up the big shots."

He quietly played this way until one critical night in 1997, when his Bulls faced the Jazz in the NBA finals. With six seconds on the clock in a tied game six, the Bulls called a timeout. Even though Jordan was recovering from the flu that night, it was obvious to everyone in the arena that the Jazz defense would swarm him if he got the ball. This might well leave the sharpshooting Kerr open.

In that moment, Kerr told me, he realized his fear wasn't just hurting his chance to shine; it was hurting the team. "I remember saying fuck it. If I get the ball I'm going to shoot it. I don't care." Sure enough, Kerr got the ball. Without a hint of hesitation, he pulled up and nailed the game and series winner. "That was the turning point in my career," he recalls.

Nearly twenty years later, when Kerr took over the Golden State Warriors as a rookie head coach, he was determined that none of his players would waste their talents feeling they had to avoid making mistakes. He would build the team's culture to assure this.

Three years later, observers consistently notice two things about Kerr's Warriors. First, a spirit of playfulness and joy infuses the team. They dance before games, laugh on the court, and take wild shots (and improbably often make them). Their performance is often compared to that of the Chicago teams Kerr played for. But led by Jordan, the Bulls were ferocious and often fueled by a fierce drive to conquer. The Warriors, by contrast, are fueled by a love of the game of basketball.

Second, the Warriors are known for winning. In year one, Kerr took the team to an NBA title, its first in forty years. In his second year, the team chased down Kerr's own 1997 Bulls for the best record in NBA history, though they were upset in the finals by LeBron James and the Cleveland Cavaliers. In year three, they avenged their loss to Cleveland, earning yet another NBA title.

Steve Kerr has intentionally worked to build a team culture that looks different from those that usually develop under high-stakes, high-stress conditions. When he talks to his players, he stresses growth over perfection. He says he works to achieve competitiveness through the intentional building of emotional maturity rather than fear of losing.

"It's really hard to be an NBA player," Kerr told me. "Sure, most people would kill to have this job. But when you think about the pressure to win, people booing you, what these guys need from us is compassion."

Kerr says he's made space for players to be themselves. He's worked to free them from the kind of anxiety he suffered as a player so they can focus completely on the game. What has followed? A love of the game, a mastery of the fundamentals (the team leads the league in offense and is near the top in defense), and a culture of experimentation. While the basketball world debates whether the Warriors are the best team ever to take the court, I'm convinced they are the most creative.

If we want those we lead to consistently practice unsafe thinking and benefit from the innovation it provides, a large body of research shows that we must intentionally craft an environment that deemphasizes hierarchy and tradition and directly encourages risk taking, self-expression, and a willingness to step out of conventional modes of operating. Kerr says that too many otherwise competent leaders fail to embrace such approaches because they haven't fully grasped that the world has changed. "The old school where the coach is the disciplinarian—those days are numbered if they're not gone already," he told me. "There are few young players who will respond to a guy yelling and screaming at him."

A few days after he described to me his "strength in numbers" philosophy, in which everyone gets to shape the culture and style of the team, I came across a surprising study that provides some solid evidence for the efficacy of Kerr's approach—allowing the group, not just the leader, to openly discuss and set norms. The study shows that by discussing ahead of time which behaviors keep our team members in a comfortable zone of interaction and which push them out, we can glean far more of a group's genius. We can access true strength in numbers.

Before I describe the study, think for a moment about the idea of political correctness and whether you think it promotes or stifles creativity. Got it? Well, Jennifer Chatman, a researcher at the University of California, Berkeley, was aware of the prevailing wisdom: restricting what language is acceptable to use limits how creative people can be. She and her colleagues decided to test if this hypothesis was in fact true.

The researchers divided study participants into several groups. Some were a mix of men and women, and some were unisex. Each group got a creative brainstorming task. But before beginning, some groups were asked to discuss the value of political correctness among themselves. This conversation had the effect of making explicit what kind of language and behavior group members found acceptable. For many of the women in the study, just having this talk raised their level of perceived safety, and thus they felt more confident expressing their ideas once the creative task began. The result: the mixed-sex groups that discussed political correctness ahead of time brainstormed significantly more novel and divergent ideas than the other groups.

We've already looked at how important it is to design groups that bring a wide mix of perspectives and life experience. Invariably, however, some members of these diverse groups will feel insecure in sharing their more outlandish and unusual ideas. For high-status members of a team, as leaders so often are, any discussion about how to make everyone feel safe and heard may seem uncomfortable, as such conversations can surface previously overlooked insensitivities. It's important to remember that these discussions will have the exact opposite effect on those who usually stand on the fringes and from whom we most need to hear.

Chatman's study might seem to conflict with what we learned about group disagreeableness. Doesn't setting norms of behavior simply pave the way for conformist thinking? The study highlights, however, that by creating a sense of safety on an interpersonal level first, we can then openly disagree and challenge each other without fearing that we'll break the bonds of group cohesion. After all, isn't it easier to argue openly with people you know will treat you with respect and appreciate you even if they disagree with your ideas?

CHAPTER 13

Rewarding the Nonobvious

How the right incentives
fuel breakthrough creative teams

W hen Steve Kerr took over as head coach of the Golden
State Warriors in 2015, the NBA team was already
one of the best in the league. The year before they
had gone a very respectable 51–31, but they had lost in the first round
of playoffs, leading to the firing of head coach Mark Jackson. Kerr knew
his first job was to acknowledge what the team was doing well, so he
showed them highlight reels from the year before, focusing on what
fans and statisticians usually notice: great shots, stunning blocks, and
athletic steals. Once he had earned their trust by showing respect for
their accomplishments, he says, he proceeded to shift the team's focus
to the important activities that usually get overlooked.

"We were last in the league in passes per game," he told me. "We
weren't involving everyone. So we started to celebrate and reward the
number of passes we made. I would read off the stats each night, and
the team got really interested. We went from 245 a game to 315, and that
had a huge impact on our ability to win."

In 2016, NBA statisticians began recording hustle stats that count
the previously unrecorded but absolutely critical factors that win games,
like shots contested, charges taken, and loose balls recovered. What
team was quickly shown to be putting in the most effort and making
the most of its raw talent? Kerr's Warriors. By celebrating not just those

who scored and made the highlight reels but those who contributed to group success, Kerr took the team from fifty-one to sixty-seven wins and an NBA title in his first season. Unfortunately, many groups, and in fact whole fields, continue to celebrate and reward only the equivalent of scoring, often with disastrous outcomes.

In 2011, Wharton's Uri Simonsohn was feeling queasy about the industry in which he had built a rather prestigious career. He and a couple of colleagues had just published a paper playfully titled "False-Positive Psychology" in which they demonstrated just how easily psychological researchers, like Simonsohn himself, find amazing effects in their studies. Want to prove that listening to certain music makes you feel older? Easy. Run the test on a number of people. If you don't like the results, add more people to the mix. Or break your subjects into groups and only report on the ones that proved your point. Such tactics may sound absurd, but they have in fact long been part of standard practice in research. Burying failure while touting success is common in the field.

The paper was interesting but not yet ground shaking; it was hardly evidence that the field was fraudulent or that researchers were intentionally fudging their results to "prove" things that actually didn't exist. Still, with so much room for manipulation, Simonsohn wondered, could we really trust decades of findings upon which our understanding of human behavior rests? He wasn't sure how to answer the question until he stumbled on a paper that seemed too good to be true.

A psychology researcher from a major university was claiming to have found an incredibly powerful correlation between people who had a physically high vantage point and a tendency toward pro-social behavior. Sure, Simonsohn thought, this correlation might be possible, but when he looked at the data, he became highly suspicious. The distribution of the researcher's findings wasn't messy like data gleaned from the real world. Instead it looked perfect, as if a teacher had given a test, and every kid's percentage score fell exactly along a bell curve.

Simonsohn began an email exchange with the paper's lead author. He prodded gently at first, wanting to give the researcher the benefit of the doubt, but before long, the house of cards came crashing down. The man retracted the article and five others citing "research errors."

For the next several years, Simonsohn turned his gaze on the data from a number of prominent studies and systematically showed that data falsification had become a widespread problem in a field supposedly dedicated to discovering objective truth.

I spoke to Simonsohn in 2016. He said he was exhausted by his work confronting fraud in his industry and no longer believed the problem could be solved by shaming the bad apples into good behavior. The problem ran deeper.

Human knowledge, Simonsohn says, advances when scientists explore at the edges of our understanding, the places where radical new ideas are often dead ends. "It's healthy to be willing to be wrong," he says. But it's also human nature to get attached to being right. "Working to build a career out of an idea and then finding evidence against it, it's like being a priest and then when you're 70 saying this whole celibacy thing was silly."

Wanting to be right is just a quirk of human nature, but the field in which these researchers work tends to magnify the problem rather than correct for it. Why? Because careers are built by publishing important findings in prestigious journals. It's downright dangerous to go too long without publication. Journals, of course, want to sell copies and grab big headlines, and that's why a recent survey found that studies showing strong positive results (proving a hypothesis) are 40 percent more likely to be published in major journals. In fact, they're 60 percent more likely to be written up at all, anywhere. That means that a tremendous amount of knowledge, interesting inquiries that didn't lead to definite positive results, simply get buried, lost to the bank of what we know.

"We need to change the field from doing research that shows things that are interesting," Simonsohn told me, "to asking questions that are interesting." But until careers can be built on interesting questions, until it's safe to pursue a bold idea that might yield a no, that change will never occur. And fraud and buried data will continue to slow the march of human understanding.

The advice that leaders should tolerate failure has been widely dispensed over the last decade. The philosophy can be implemented superficially by touting the ethic and not coming down too hard on those who fail. But making space for real risk taking is far thornier than that. Science has been touting failure tolerance since the beginning of the scientific revolution: experiment, be objective, push the boundaries, commit to the truth not the idea. Simonsohn is just the latest rebel to show how inadequate that philosophy is as long as the incentives don't match it.

Seeking to understand how leaders can actually make it safe to ask the big questions and step into the unknown, I discovered the work of the Center for Open Science (COS), which is picking the problem apart with scientific rigor. The policies COS promotes are specific to the problem it is trying to crack. A major initiative is preregistration in which questions and research methods are defined and publicly announced before study data are analyzed to reduce bias in data collection. COS is also partnering with journals to use "registered reports" in which the journal "peer-reviews" a research project's design before it starts and, if the project passes, agrees to publish the results regardless of outcomes. As more scientists and journals commit to COS's guidelines, it becomes more and more possible for researchers to build reputations for the brilliance of their curiosity and boldness of their ideas rather than their ability to project an air of infallibility.

Andrew Sallans, COS's director of operations, told me getting the incentives just right requires lots of trial and error and continuous feedback from the community.

To instill a sense in our teams that it's safe to take risks, a focus on incentives that reward effort and not just results is critical. How people build esteem and power in an organization or a field says far more than any proclaimed philosophy. It's just natural for leaders to reward wins, not process, and that means in most enterprises there's plenty of work to do to counterbalance the message this sends. While COS's work shows there's no preset formula for proper incentives, research indicates that we can begin by specifically rewarding contributors who pursue thoughtful but disruptive lines of experimentation (regardless of where they lead). We can give credit to those who share their negative results, recognizing that in doing so they're saving the larger group from repeating their mistakes. And we can provide incentives based on group rather than individual performance, allowing for some members to risk hitting dead ends while still sharing in the larger group's success.

A couple of years ago I went to visit a friend who worked at GoogleX, an incubator that tasks visionaries with inventing the future. We sat out on a sunny patio as prototypes of self-driving vehicles quietly whirred by. We couldn't talk about the specifics of his work, which was too secret for him to discuss. Instead, we talked about what it was like to work at an organization that gave one the freedom to pursue just about anything.

My friend, a graduate of MIT and Stanford, looked over his shoulder before saying, "Here, so many of us suffer from impostor syndrome. We've done surveys and most of us don't think we're as smart as our colleagues. A lot of times, I actually wind up holding ideas back because I don't want to come off as stupid."

Even in an organization known for its focus on experimentation and intentional culture building, where some of the world's smartest, most confident inventors come to create, I found a lack of self-assurance putting limits on creativity. Groups, this conversation reminded me, must be constantly cultivated to allow for disruption as well as invited and incentivized to step beyond the bounds of safety. And that takes a constant focus from leaders at all levels.

When it's done right, the payoff is profound. The year 2017 was an enormously difficult one for Steve Kerr. The effects of a back surgery gone wrong left him in long-term excruciating pain. By the time the playoffs rolled around, he was not even able to show up on the court. He handed the team over to an assistant. But the Warriors hardly missed a beat. They won fifteen games in a row to start the playoffs on the way to a 16–1 run to a championship. The joyful, creative approach Kerr inspired isn't dependent on him. It's a group effort. Every player on the team contributes to keeping the Warriors' culture on its creative edge.

LEADERSHIP: KEY TAKEAWAYS

Resist quick-forming consensus

When people get together, they tend to magnify the problems of safe thinking. They overweight the ideas of leaders, punish outliers, and rush to conclusions. But groups with disagreeable people who encourage productive conflict can escape these traps. If disagreement isn't flowing easily, gamify it with tools like prediction markets and red teams.

What do you do to disrupt the agreeableness of the teams you work on? Remember, doing it well means doing it with kindness and respect. Do you invite ideas from the edges and share them when you have them? If you're a leader, remember that shared information bias is weakened when leaders listen first and invite everyone to speak.

Make getting unsafe safe

People are more likely to act and think in unsafe ways when the environment around them is safe. The study on political correctness demonstrated that creating a welcoming and protective environment didn't depress group creativity but enhanced it. And Steve Kerr found success by lowering the stress levels of his pressure-cooked NBA players.

As a leader do you work to make sure everyone feels safe enough to take risks? Ask lower-status individuals in your organization what holds them back. You're likely to discover that a few tweaks can release a lot of creativity.

Incentivize risk taking, not just success

How people gain status, money, and esteem in an organization says more than any policy or stated philosophy. The Center for Open Science is repairing a broken research culture not by lecturing scientists on how to behave but by changing the incentives of the field. Once careers can be built on exploration and good questions, not just definitive discoveries, far more risk taking becomes possible.

Do you reward those you lead for things other than success? Directly incentivize other key activities like taking intelligent risks, reporting failures, and posing smart questions. This can redirect teams away from conservative approaches and into the unknown.

Epilogue

t was November 3, 2008, the day before Election Day in the United States, and a middle-aged woman sat at her desk in central New Jersey. She had registered to vote, meaning that at some point she had intended to exercise her right to help choose her elected officials. Still, the data tells us, there was only a 47 percent chance that she would actually show up at the polls. For the time being, her mind was elsewhere, as she casually scrolled through her Facebook feed.

Distracted by a vaguely worded offer to complete a survey, the woman clicked and found that, like everything else these days, the survey was election related. The ten questions were bland. Most of them asked her some variation of "How important is it to you to vote in the upcoming election?" She answered each one, and when she was done, she returned to her feed.

Maybe it was the extra reminder that tomorrow was Election Day or maybe it had to do with being prompted to think about how important voting is, but there was now, researchers discovered, a 79 percent chance that this woman would cast a vote.

It was an impressive impact but hardly unexpected. It's long been understood that if you prompt someone to think about voting just before Election Day, they're more likely to vote. The researchers thought they could push the effect much further.

That same day, a second version of the survey went out on social media. The same vague invitation, ten bland questions. This time, however, the wording was just a little different. This survey asked several variations on the question "How important is it to you to be a voter in the upcoming election?" See the switch? Now the experimenters weren't asking people how important it was to vote but how important it was to "be a voter." The impact of the subtle wording change was enormous: 90 percent of those who got questions phrased this way got out of their chairs and went to the polls. Think of the impact of the grammatical change this way: out of those who took the first survey, 20 percent were still willing to skip the election, but half as many laggards emerged from the second, nearly identical survey.

The effect of the linguistic shift from "to vote" to "be a voter" was "among the largest experimental effects ever observed on objectively measured voter turnout," according to the experimenters, who came from the University of Chicago, Harvard, and Stanford.

◇◇◇◇◇◇◇◇

This is a book about changing well-worn habits of thinking and behaving, and habit change is exceedingly difficult. Whether the goal is to broaden our thinking, master new disciplines, or just get to the gym, we all get stuck in ruts. But we can change behavior, experiments like this and many similar ones show, when we create positive images of ourselves that we strive to live up to. The voting experimenters note that our sense of self can play a key role in shaping our behavior and that the self is a continual work in progress. When we're induced to think of ourselves as voters, we naturally ask, What would a voter do in this situation? And then we go out and vote, even when taking that action is inconvenient or difficult.

The internal role models we create are some of the most powerful tools we possess for changing ourselves when we need to do so most. My research into unsafe thinking has shown me, however, that many of us (myself included) have been walking around with the wrong kinds of role models in our heads, stereotypes from a bygone era that no longer serve us.

I've discovered that the most courageous leaders aren't above feeling fear and anxiety; they allow themselves to feel it and are fueled by it. The most valuable thinkers aren't infallible experts; they are eager explorers, willing to admit when they've been wrong and to update and revise their thinking as new evidence emerges. Visionary creatives don't draw their inspiration magically from unquestioned gut feel; they learn to rely on but also to test and hone their intuition, using their analytical minds to make their intuitive senses sharper. Those who fight most effectively to change the world for the better don't judge and shun those who oppose them but allow their foes into their circles of influence and learn to benefit from the uncomfortable perspectives they offer. And the most valuable contributors to a team are not necessarily those who generate the answers and influence others to follow; they are often the ones who draw out the ideas from the edges and create an environment safe enough for the genius of a group to emerge.

It seems to me that so many conventional notions of what it means to be a leader, a creator, or a disruptor are just plain wrong. If we want to adapt to a changing world, we need to attune our internal role models to the latest science and to our times. So, while I hope you've highlighted and noted dozens of specific insights and ways to practice the nonobvious approaches I've called unsafe thinking, perhaps the most important thing you can do is try confronting challenging situations with a new internal role model, to ask yourself when you face the unknown, What would an unsafe thinker do? And then do it.

◇◇◇◇◇◇◇◇

Here's what happened when I asked that question. It was Christmas Eve. My wife and I were in Los Angeles, where we had gone to get away from the all-consuming work I had been doing to reinject creativity and joy into my company. Because we had implemented many of the unsafe thinking principles I had been studying, and because I had relied on them for my own leadership development, our crisis had largely passed. A sense of stability and pride was returning to the office. I felt the exhaustion of having rolled an enormous boulder up a hill and the recognition that, like all CEOs, I would no doubt have to do it all over again sometime soon.

As we walked down a city beach, our kids running ahead into the waves, my phone rang. There was a new fire to put out, and, no, it couldn't wait until the holiday was over. I set the phone down, and instead of jumping right into problem-solving mode, I asked myself, What would an unsafe thinker do? My immediate response wasn't the one I would have expected, and it had little to do with the problem I had just been handed over the phone. For seventeen years, my core identity had formed around this company I had built. Its successes were my successes; its failures, my failures. I'd never had another job and never intended to. But when I asked myself that simple question, the answer was clear: Let go.

"I think I've done all I can do," I said to my wife, and I could tell by the look she immediately gave me that she had already known this for some time.

For the past year, I had spent every moment I could steal studying how people challenged and changed themselves, how they confronted their deepest conservatism, their sense of self, and their strongest beliefs. I learned from each of them, in their own way, that challenging the outside world becomes possible when we get comfortable challenging ourselves.

It became clear when I asked that question that stepping down as CEO, passing the company on to new leaders, and facing the unknown was the challenge I now most needed to take on. With a conviction that new creative possibilities awaited me on the outside, my reasons for staying in the spot where I'd always stood—stability, ego, continuity—felt like nothing but safe thinking.

By adopting a new internal role model, by striving to live up to my own personal image of an unsafe thinker, I was able to take the next necessary step in my creative evolution—a step I had once believed I could never take. I hope unsafe thinking will allow you, in your own way, to do the same.

ACKNOWLEDGMENTS

Unsafe Thinking began as a nebulous set of questions and interviews about how to increase one's creativity while under pressure. In 2015, I wasn't just musing about this topic in an abstract way. I was under a lot of pressure and not feeling quite creative enough to respond effectively.

I was fortunate enough to find my way to Emily Loose, who helped me craft these questions into the outlines of a book. She stuck with me every step of the way, pushing my thinking and my writing, reassuring me when I felt lost, and deeply enriching my understanding of what it takes to create a worthwhile read. There would be no book without her.

I am also immeasurably grateful to my agent, Joy Tutela of the David Black Agency, and Dan Ambrosio, my editor at Da Capo, who believed in this project enough to bring it to reality while being critical enough to make it far sharper. Megan Lardner, as my research assistant, brilliantly took my vague assignments and dug up compelling stories that brought the science in this book to life.

I benefitted from the sharp eye, critical questions, and insightful suggestions of my early readers, including Ari Derfel, Nigel Wilcoxson, Phil Kim, Mary Childs, Stephan Flothmann, Jeff Kirschner, Siggy Rubinson, Collin West, Emily Sachs, Nancy Kantor-Hodge, and Nigel Hodge.

When I set out to research this book, I held out hope that important academics and practitioners would take the time to speak with me, though I had little reason to believe they would. I was amazed by the generosity of so many luminary thinkers who gave me their time. A partial list of them includes Jason Klein, Teresa Amabile, John Mackey,

Micah White, Julie Wainwright, Cam McLeay, Mihaly Csikszentmihalyi, Krtin Nithiyanandam, Philip Tetlock, Erik Dane, Laura Huang, Candida Brush, Trish Costello, Robin Hogarth, Clint Korver, Erik Swartz, Barry Marshall, Ira Chaleff, Joan Blades, Reverend Jeffrey Brown, Jeffrey Kassing, Steve Kerr, Uri Simonsohn, Andrew Sallans, Mia Consolvo, Ed Catmull, Will Le, Cindy Odhiambo, Margaret Adoyo Rachuonyo, Wilfreda Agul Oketch, Bob Berman, Rohit Bhargava, Udaya Patnaik, Burt Dorman, Edward Miguel, Danny Friedlander, Mark Youngblood, Jeff DeGraff, Roger Schank, Matthew Peskay, Vicki Abeles, Matan Yaffe, Carissa Carter, Rex Jung, Justin Rosenstein, Carl Sparks, Tony Hsieh, Tyler Williams, Daniel Deng, Daniel Souweine, Randy Haykin, Mark Culvert, Peter Sims, Dan Cohen, and Erica Berger.

Finally, none of my creative endeavors would be possible without the love and support of my family: Chelsea, Mira, and Orion. Thank you for giving me the space, the confidence, and the foundation I need to follow my questions to answers.

NOTES

Prologue

The story of the Hartford Yard Goats came to me through conversations with Jason Klein as well as from Kristin Hussey, "Hartford Yard Goats? The Name Isn't a Hit Yet," *New York Times*, June 28, 2015, https://www.nytimes.com/2015/06/29/nyregion /hartford-yard-goats-the-name-isnt-a-hit-yet.html.

Introduction

Medical surveys show that when doctors recommend critical lifestyle changes, up to 70 percent of us choose to stick to our comfortable, unhealthy ways. Leslie R. Martin et al., "The Challenge of Patient Adherence," *Therapeutics and Clinical Risk Management*, September 2005, https://www.ncbi.nlm.nih.gov/pmc/articles/PMC1661624/#b17.

Gallup reports that more than two-thirds of Americans are disengaged at work. "Employee Engagement in U.S. Stagnant in 2015," Gallup, http://www.gallup.com /poll/188144/employee-engagement-stagnant-2015.aspx.

For more on Amabile's componential theory of creativity, see Teresa Amabile, "Componential Theory of Creativity" (Working Paper 12-096, Harvard Business School, April 26, 2012), http://www.hbs.edu/faculty/Publication%20Files/12-096.pdf.

Chapter 1

Whole Foods: "PETA Sues Whole Foods over 'Humane Meat' Claims," PETA, September 21, 2015, https://www.peta.org/blog/peta-sues-whole-foods-over-humane-meat -claims; Stephanie Stromjune, "Whole Foods Accused of Overcharging in New York City Stores," *New York Times*, June 25, 2015, https://www.nytimes.com/2015/06/25 /business/whole-foods-accused-of-overcharging-in-new-york-city-stores.html.

In test after test, only about 3 percent of people can crack the cheap necklace problem. E. Fioratou, R. Flin, and R. Glavin, "No Simple Fix for Fixation Errors: Cognitive Processes and Their Clinical Application," *Anaesthesia* 65 (2010): 61–69.

Thomas Edison, ingeniously, found a way to harness the creative power of extremely low arousal states. Jeffrey Kluger, "The Spark of Invention," Time.com, November 14, 2013, http://techland.time.com/2013/11/14/the-spark-of-invention.

When people who had faced social exclusion were interviewed, nearly all of them said they would rather have experienced physical abuse than ostracism. Beth Azar, "Singled Out: Social Rejection and Ostracism Are Emerging as Powerful Psychological Forces That Shape Human Behavior in Positive and Negative Ways," *Monitor on Psychology* 40, no. 4 (2009), http://www.apa.org/monitor/2009/04/social.aspx.

Chapter 2

I base my retelling of Gandhi's story primarily on the following sources: Eknath Easwaran, *Gandhi the Man: How One Man Changed Himself to Change the World*, 4th ed. (Tomales, CA: Nilgiri Press, 2011); Mahatma Gandhi, *The Essential Gandhi: An Anthology of His Writings on His Life, Work, and Ideas* (New York: Vintage, 1983); Mohandas Karamchand Gandhi, *Gandhi: An Autobiography: The Story of My Experiments with the Truth* (Boston: Beacon Press, 1993).

For more on Steven Hayes and his theory of experiential avoidance, see Steven C. Hayes, *Get Out of Your Mind and Into Your Life: The New Acceptance and Commitment Therapy* (Oakland, CA: New Harbinger Publications, 2005).

Those trying not to feel anxious not only failed to avoid anxiety but had a worse experience of the feared event when it did arrive. Michael J. L. Sullivan et al., "Thought Suppression, Catastrophizing, and Pain," *Cognitive Therapy and Research* 21, no. 5 (October 1997): 555–568, https://link.springer.com/article/10.1023/A:1021809519002.

Micah White is cofounder of the Occupy Wall Street movement. Eric Westervelt, "Occupy Activist Micah White: Time to Move Beyond Memes and Street Spectacles," National Public Radio, March 28, 2017, http://www.npr.org/2017/03/28/520911740 /occupy-activist-micah-white-time-to-move-beyond-memes-and-street-spectacles.

Chapter 3

My telling of Julie Wainwright's story comes primarily from my interview with her and from Michelle Quinn, "From Pets.com's Sock Puppet to Lightly Worn Prada, CEO Makes a Comeback," *San Jose Mercury News*, October 3, 2016, http:// www.mercurynews.com/2016/10/03/from-pets-coms-sock-puppet-to-lightly-worn -prada-ceo-makes-a-comeback.

The London School of Economics studied fifty-one companies using pay-for-performance plans and found that these bonuses actually decreased employee effectiveness. "When Performance-Related Pay Backfires," London School of Economics, http://www .lse.ac.uk/website-archive/newsAndMedia/news/archives/2009/06/performancepay.aspx.

Studies of fine artists have rated the paintings they were paid to do as significantly less creative than their noncommissioned works. Teresa Amabile, *Creativity in Context: Update to The Social Psychology of Creativity* (Boulder, CO: Westview Press, 1996).

My retelling of Harry Harlow's motivation experiments was guided by the excellent account in Daniel Pink, *Drive: The Surprising Truth About What Motivates Us* (New York City: Riverhead Books, 2011).

I draw my account of the Atlanta Public Schools cheating scandal from Dana Goldstein, "How High-Stakes Testing Led to the Atlanta Cheating Scandal," *Slate*, July 2011, http://www.slate.com/articles/double_x/doublex/2011/07/how_highstakes_testing_led_to_the_atlanta_cheating_scandal.html; Rachel Aviv, "Wrong Answer: In an era of High-Stakes Testing, a Struggling School Made a Shocking Choice," *New Yorker*, July 21, 2014, http://www.newyorker.com/contributors/rachel-aviv.

For more on the study that inoculated children against the disadvantages of extrinsic motivation, see Beth A. Hennessey and Susan M. Zbikowski, "Immunizing Children Against the Negative Effects of Reward: A Further Examination of Intrinsic Motivation Training Techniques," *Creativity Research Journal* 6, no. 3 (1993).

For John Cleese's talk on creativity, see "John Cleese on Creativity in Management," video posted to YouTube by Video Arts on June 21, 2017, https://www.youtube.com/watch?v=Pb5oIIPO62g.

Chapter 4

My account of the Ascend the Nile expedition comes from my conversations with Cam McLeay, his personal diaries, and Stefan Lovgren, "Nile Explorers Battled Adversity, Tragedy to Find River Source," *National Geographic News*, April 19, 2006, http://news.nationalgeographic.com/news/2006/04/0419_060419_nile_2.html.

My source for flow theory is primarily *Flow: The Psychology of Optimal Experience* (New York: HarperCollins, 2009).

John Irving's description of the experience of his work comes via Teresa Amabile, "How to Kill Creativity," *Harvard Business Review*, September 1998, https://hbr.org/1998/09/how-to-kill-creativity.

For more on the experiments to sample flow experience with pagers, see R. Larson and M. Csikszentmihalyi, "The Experience Sampling Method," *New Directions for Methodology of Social and Behavioral Science* 15 (1983): 41–56.

For Joshua Foer's discussion of the OK Plateau, see Joshua Foer, "Step Outside Your Comfort Zone and Study Yourself Failing," 99U, http://99u.com/videos/7061/joshua-foer-step-outside-your-comfort-zone-and-study-yourself-failing.

Participants chose electric shocks over quiet contemplation: Timothy D. Wilson et al., "Just Think: The Challenges of the Disengaged Mind," *Science* 345, no. 6192 (July 4, 2014): 75–77.

"Survey Shows Millennials Are More Forgetful Than Seniors," *Business Wire*, http://www.businesswire.com/news/home/20130801006048/en/Survey-Shows-Millennials-Forgetful-Seniors.

On the cost of distraction at work, see "Social Media Distractions Cost U.S. Economy $650 Billion [INFOGRAPHIC]," *Mashable*, http://mashable.com/2012/11/02/social-media-work-productivity/#zLi_pIKfqEqt.

For more on the Carnegie Mellon study on the effects of distraction, see Bob Sullivan and Hugh Thompson, "Brain, Interrupted Gray Matter," *New York Times*, May 3, 2013, http://www.nytimes.com/2013/05/05/opinion/sunday/a-focus-on-distraction.html.

Jonathan Franzen's recommendations for maintaining focus come from Lev Grossman, "Jonathan Franzen: Great American Novelist," *Time*, August 12, 2010, http://content.time.com/time/magazine/article/0,9171,2010185,00.html.

E. Paul Torrance, "The Importance of Falling in Love with Something," ResearchGate, January 1, 1983, https://www.researchgate.net/publication/232474524_The_importance_of_falling_in_love_with_something.

Chapter 5

The science of the exam nightmare is discussed in more depth at Janice Paskey, "Exam Nightmares," McGill, http://news-archive.mcgill.ca/f95/4.htm.

The authors of a recent survey of Nobel Prize winners explained the huge concentration of laureates who did their prize-worthy work in their thirties. The average age was thirty-six. Benjamin Jones, E. J. Reedy, and Bruce A. Weinberg, "Age and Scientific Genius" (Working Paper 19866, National Bureau of Economic Research, January 2014), http://www.nber.org/papers/w19866.pdf.

My account of Nithiyanandam's Alzheimer's breakthrough comes from personal conversations and from the following: "Scientific American Innovator Award—Krtin Nithiyanandam—Google Science Fair 2015," video posted to YouTube by Google Science Fair on February 13, 2016, https://www.youtube.com/watch?v=c67HkyQfr78; Sarah Knapton, "15-Year-Old Schoolboy Develops Test for Alzheimer's Disease," *Telegraph*, July 13, 2015, http://www.telegraph.co.uk/news/science/science-news/11734666/15-year-old-schoolboy-develops-test-for-Alzheimers-disease.html.

For an excellent summation of Erik Dane's research on entrenchment, see E. Dane, "Reconsidering the Trade-off Between Expertise and Flexibility: A Cognitive Entrenchment Perspective," *Academy of Management Review* 35, no. 4 (October 1, 2010): 579–603.

Sigmund Freud: "The conceptions I have summarized here I first put forward only tentatively, but in the course of time they have won such a hold over me that I can no longer think in any other way." Sigmund Freud, *Civilization and Its Discontents* (New York: W. W. Norton & Company, 2010).

Insights from Gary Klein on expert intuition come from Gary Klein, *Seeing What Others Don't: The Remarkable Ways We Gain Insights* (New York: PublicAffairs, 2013).

Philip Tetlock's insights into expertise come from my conversation with him and from these sources: Philip E. Tetlock, *Expert Political Judgment: How Good Is It? How Can We Know?* (Princeton, NJ: Princeton University Press, 2015); Louis Menand, "Everybody's an Expert: Putting Predictions to the Test," *New Yorker*, December 5, 2005.

W. W. Maddux and A. D. Galinsky, "Cultural Borders and Mental Barriers: Living in and Adapting to Foreign Cultures Facilitates Creativity" (Working Paper No. 2007/51/ OB, INSEAD, Fontainebleau, France, September 2007).

Information on Mick Pearce's design for the Eastgate Center comes from Abigail Doan, "Biomimetic Architecture: Green Building in Zimbabwe Modeled After Termite Mounds," Inhabitat.com, 2012, http://inhabitat.com/building-modelled-on-termites -eastgate-centre-in-zimbabwe; Tom McKeag, "How Termites Inspired Mick Pearce's Green Building," *Greenbiz*, 2009, https://www.greenbiz.com/blog/2009/09/02/how -termites-inspired-mick-pearces-green-buildings.

For an in-depth account of Abraham Wald's story and more on the math behind his insights, see Jordan Ellenberg, *How Not to Be Wrong: The Power of Mathematical Thinking* (New York: Penguin, 2014).

Chapter 6

The story of Vineet Nayar's humbling dance comes from the following sources: Vineet Nayar, "How I Did It: A Maverick CEO Explains How He Persuaded His Team to Leap into the Future," *Harvard Business Review*, June 2010, https://hbr.org/2010/06 /how-i-did-it-a-maverick-ceo-explains-how-he-persuaded-his-team-to-leap-into -the-future; "Vineet Nayyar @ Directions 2011 HCL," video posted to YouTube by Kaly- an Maruvada, November 10, 2010, https://www.youtube.com/watch?v=S0N1UkUgefc.

For the study that shows how believing you're an expert makes you more prone to error, see Stav Atir, Emily Rosenzweig, and David Dunning, "When Knowledge Knows No Bounds: Self-Perceived Expertise Predicts Claims of Impossible Knowledge," *Psychological Science* 26, no. 8 (July 14, 2015): 1295–1303.

Studies on the better-than-average effect include Ezra W. Zuckerman and John T. Jost, "What Makes You Think You're So Popular? Self-Evaluation Maintenance and the Subjective Side of the 'Friendship Paradox,'" *Social Psychology Quarterly* 64, no. 3 (September 2001): 207–223; Constantine Sedikides et al., "Behind Bars but Above the Bar: Prisoners Consider Themselves More Prosocial Than Non-prisoners," *British Journal of Social Psychology* 53, no. 2 (December 23, 2013); C. E. Preston and S. Harris, "Psychology of Drivers in Traffic Accidents," *Journal of Applied Psychology* 49, no. 4 (August 1965): 284–288.

For Jimmy Cayne's comments leading up to the collapse of Bear Stearns, see Mal- colm Gladwell, "Cocksure Banks, Battles, and the Psychology of Overconfidence," *New Yorker*, July 27, 2009.

My account of the demise of Nokia comes from Roger Cheng, "Farewell Nokia: The Rise and Fall of a Mobile Pioneer," CNET, April 25, 2014, https://www.cnet.com /news/farewell-nokia-the-rise-and-fall-of-a-mobile-pioneer.

Instead of making their employees feel uncertain and unguided, humble leaders, according to a 2013 study from the University of Washington and State University of New York, Buffalo, were far more likely to have engaged, satisfied, and loyal employees. Bradley P. Owens, Michael D. Johnson, and Terrence R. Mitchell, "Expressed Humility in Organizations: Implications for Performance, Teams, and Leadership," *Organization Science* 24, no. 5 (2013): 1517–1538.

Jim March's account of his consulting comes from Diane Coutu, "Ideas as Art," *Harvard Business Review*, October 2010, https://hbr.org/2006/10/ideas-as-art.

My account of Elaine Bromiley's death and her husband's reform crusade comes from Ian Leslie, "How Mistakes Can Save Lives: One Man's Mission to Revolutionise the NHS," *New Statesman*, June 4, 2014.

For the blurred-image recognition experiment, see Jerome S. Bruner and Mary C. Potter, "Interference in Visual Recognition," *Science*, n.s., 144, no. 3617 (April 24, 1964): 424–425.

My coverage of the psychological tendency to "seize and freeze" was informed by Arie W. Kruglanski and Donna M. Webster, "Motivated Closing of the Mind: 'Seizing' and 'Freezing,'" *Psychological Review* 103, no. 2 (1996): 263–283.

One fascinating study that demonstrates the difficulty of dislodging a preliminary judgment comes from Barbara O'Brien, "Prime Suspect: An Examination of Factors That Aggravate and Counteract Confirmation Bias in Criminal Investigations," *Psychology, Public Policy, and Law* 15, no. 4 (2009): 315–334; Barbara O'Brien, "A Recipe for Bias: An Empirical Look at the Interplay Between Institutional Incentives and Bounded Rationality in Prosecutorial Decision Making," *Missouri Law Review* 74, no. 4 (fall 2009): 999.

Chapter 7

For Robert J. Sternberg's investment theory of creativity, see "Investment Theory of Creativity," Robert J. Sternberg, http://www.robertjsternberg.com/investment -theory-of-creativity.

A 2014 survey of more than 1,000 executives found that business leaders relied most often on intuition, beating out data and the advice of others. Economist Intelligence Unit, "Guts and Gigabytes," PWC, 2015, https://www.pwc.com/gx/en/issues /data-and-analytics/big-decisions-survey/assets/big-decisions2014.pdf.

A discussion of intuition as subconscious analysis can be found at Alden M. Hayashi, "When to Trust Your Gut," *Harvard Business Review*, February 2001, https:// hbr.org/2001/02/when-to-trust-your-gut.

For further reading on Kahneman and Tversky's research on heuristics and System 1/System 2 thinking, see Daniel Kahneman, *Thinking Fast and Slow* (New York: Farrar, Straus and Giroux, 2013).

Examples of the genius of intuition come from the following sources: the Formula One race car driver: University of Leeds, "Go with Your Gut—Intuition Is More Than Just a Hunch, Says New Research," ScienceDaily.com, March 6, 2008, www.science daily.com/releases/2008/03/080305144210.htm; quote from Wolfgang Amadeus Mozart: Irving Singer, *Modes of Creativity: Philosophical Perspectives* (Boston: MIT Press 2010); the Tel Aviv numeric averaging study: "Going with Your Gut: Decision Making Based on Instinct Alone 90% Accurate of the Time, Study Shows," ZME

Science, November 2012, http://www.zmescience.com/research/studies/decision-making-intuition-accurate-42433.

My coverage of Laura Huang's research comes from a conversation with her as well as Laura Huang and Jone L. Pearce, "Managing the Unknowable: The Effectiveness of Early-stage Investor Gut Feel in Entrepreneurial Investment Decisions," *Administrative Science Quarterly* 60, no. 4 (July 16, 2015): 634–670, http://journals.sagepub.com/doi/pdf/10.1177/0001839215597270.

Allison Woods Brooks et al., "Investors Prefer Entrepreneurial Ventures Pitched by Attractive Men," PNAS 111, no. 12 (March 25, 2014): 4427–4431, http://www.pnas.org/content/111/12/4427.full.pdf.

Statistics on gender bias in investing are drawn from my conversation with Candida Brush and Candida G. Brush et al., "Diana Report: Women Entrepreneurs 2014: Bridging the Gender Gap in Venture Capital," Arthur M. Blank Center for Entrepreneurship, Babson College, September 2014.

Chapter 8

More than two-thirds of respondents said that k is more often the first than the third letter in English words. In truth a typical English text contains twice the number of words with k in the third position. Amos Tversky and Daniel Kahneman, "Availability: A Heuristic for Judging Frequency and Probability," *Cognitive Psychology* 5 (1973): 207–232, https://msu.edu/~ema/803/Ch11-JDM/2/TverskyKahneman73.pdf.

For more information on familiarity bias in investment behavior, see Gur Huberman, "Familiarity Breeds Investment" (New York: Columbia University, 2000).

For Sarah Nadav's plea to stop comparing female entrepreneurs to investors' wives, see Sarah Nadav, "VCs—Don't Compare Me to Your Wife, Just Don't," Beyourself, February 2016, https://byrslf.co/vcs-don-t-compare-me-to-your-wife-just-don-t-9dc2c8c1ac93.

Sources for the story of An Wang and the demise of his company include Bart Ziegler, "Once-Booming Wang Laboratories Failed to Heed the Changing Market," Associated Press, August 23, 1992, http://community.seattletimes.nwsource.com/archive/?date=19920823&slug=1508984; Dennis Hevesi, "An Wang, 70, Is Dead of Cancer; Inventor and Maker of Computers," *New York Times*, March 25, 1990, http://www.nytimes.com/1990/03/25/obituaries/an-wang-70-is-dead-of-cancer-inventor-and-maker-of-computers.html; Myrna Oliver, "An Wang; Founded Computer Company," *Los Angeles Times*, March 25, 1990, http://articles.latimes.com/1990-03-25/news/mn-214_1_wang-laboratories.

The danger of our emotions' misleading us is put into stark relief by some recent research about how being in tune with our feelings while making a judgment affects our actions. Barnaby D. Dunn et al., "Listening to Your Heart: How Interoception Shapes Emotion Experience and Intuitive Decision Making," *Psychological Science* 21, no. 12 (November 24, 2010): 1835–1844.

Robin Hogarth's ideas on honing intuition are drawn from our conversations and from Robin Hogarth, *Educating Intuition* (Chicago: University of Chicago Press, 2010).

For the study on how to effectively reduce unconscious bias, see Nilanjana Dasgupta and Anthony G. Greenwald, "On the Malleability of Automatic Attitudes: Combating Automatic Prejudice with Images of Admired and Disliked Individuals," *Journal of Personality and Social Psychology* 81, no. 5 (2001): 800–814, https://faculty.washington.edu/agg/pdf/Dasgupta_Gwald._JPSP_2001.OCR.pdf.

Harvard psychologist Mahzarin Banaji, who has made a career of studying unconscious bias, invented a brilliant trick to do. She installed a screensaver on her computer that flashes images of all sorts of people that counter stereotypes, such as of short bald men who are executives. Mahzarin R. Banaji and Anthony G. Greenwald, *Blindspot: Hidden Biases of Good People* (New York: Random House 2016).

For more on the incentive to keep donors uninformed of specific outcomes, see Paul Niehaus, "A Theory of Good Intentions," University of California, San Diego, June 21, 2014, http://econweb.ucsd.edu/~pniehaus/papers/good_intentions.pdf.

Chapter 9

The story of Antanas Mockus comes from the following sources: "Cities on Speed: The Inspiring Story of Antanas Mockus," video posted to YouTube by Duval Guimaraes, April 3, 2013, https://www.youtube.com/watch?v=33-4NRpowF8; Ray Fisman and Edward Miguel, *Economic Gangsters: Corruption, Violence, and the Poverty of Nations* (Princeton, NJ: Princeton University Press, 2010); Antanas Mockus, "The Art of Changing a City," *New York Times*, July 17, 2015, https://www.nytimes.com/2015/07/17/opinion/the-art-of-changing-a-city.html.

For the story of Marilyn vos Savant and the Monty Hall problem, see Zachary Crockett, "The Time Everyone 'Corrected' the World's Smartest Woman," Priceonomics, https://priceonomics.com/the-time-everyone-corrected-the-worlds-smartest; "Game Show Problem," Marilyn vos Savant, http://marilynvossavant.com/game-show-problem.

For a description of how Einstein found insight through visualization, see Walter Isaacson, "The Light-Beam Rider," *New York Times*, October 30, 2015, https://www.nytimes.com/2015/11/01/opinion/sunday/the-light-beam-rider.html.

For the tragic story of Kenney Bui, see Lee Carpenter, "Kenney Bui: The Life and Death of a High School Football Player," *Guardian*, October 14, 2015, https://www.theguardian.com/sport/2015/oct/14/kenney-bui-high-school-football; Jabarnett13, "Kenney Bui of Evergreen (Wash.) Dies of On-Field Football Injury," *USA Today*, October 5, 2015, http://usatodayhss.com/2015/seattle-football-injuries-tackling-head-neck.

Football has always been a dangerous sport. As the game began to reach national prominence in the 1960s and players got stronger, faster, and more determined to achieve fame, the number of deaths from brain injuries began to climb from already unacceptably high levels. Between 1965 and 1969 more than one hundred players died—that's a rate of about twenty per year. Whet Moser, "A Brief History of Football Head Injuries and a Look Toward the Future," *Chicago Magazine*, May 2013, http://www.chicagomag.com/Chicago-Magazine/The-312/May-2012/A-Brief-History-of-Football-Head-Injuries-and-a-Look-Towards-the-Future.

I learned about Erik Swartz's intervention in football safety through conversations with him and from Terrence McCoy, "The Counterintuitive Idea That Could Drastically Reduce Head Injuries in Football," *Washington Post*, January 8, 2016, https://www.washingtonpost.com/news/inspired-life/wp/2016/01/08/the-counter-intuitive-idea-that-could-drastically-reduce-head-injuries-in-football.

For a rich academic discussion of minimally counterintuitive concepts, see M. Afzal Upal, "On Attractiveness of Surprising Ideas: How Memory for Counterintuitive Ideas Drives Cultural Dynamics," Academia.edu, http://www.academia.edu/12852275/On_Attractiveness_of_Surprising_Ideas_How_Memory_for_Counter intuitive_Ideas_Drives_Cultural_Dynamics.

Chapter 10

The story of Paul Buchheit and the birth of Gmail comes primarily from Harry McCracken, "How Gmail Happened: The Inside Story of Its Launch 10 Years Ago," *Time*, April 1, 2014, http://time.com/43263/gmail-10th-anniversary.

For Francesca Gino's study on how cheating makes us more creative, see Francesca Gino and Dan Ariely, "The Dark Side of Creativity: Original Thinkers Can Be More Dishonest," *Journal of Personality and Social Psychology* 102, no. 3 (2012): 445–459.

Arizona State's Zhen Zhang also found a consistent correlation between a tendency to break rules and creative success later in life. Among the white male subjects he studied, minor infractions committed in adolescence—like playing hooky and defacing property—predicted much higher chances of becoming a successful entrepreneur later in life. Jenna Pincott, "Are These Rules Worth Breaking?," *Psychology Today*, November 2014, https://www.psychologytoday.com/articles/201411/are-these-rules-worth-breaking.

For the study on teachers' attitudes toward creative students, see Erik L. Wesby and V. L. Dawson, "Creativity: Asset or Burden in the Classroom?," *Creativity Research Journal* 8, no. 1 (1995), http://www.tandfonline.com/doi/abs/10.1207/s1532 6934crj0801_1.

Barry Marshall's story came to me via my direct conversations with him as well as the following press coverage: Alex B. Berezow, "Mad Scientists of the Modern Age: Barry Marshall," *Real Clear Science*, October 2012, http://www.realclearscience.com/blog/2012/10/mad-scientists-of-the-modern-age-barry-marshall.html; Vikki Hufnagel, "Why I Elected to Give My Stories to the National Enquirer," Drvikki.com, October 2015, http://www.drvikki.com/why-the-enquirer.html; Lawrence Altman, "New Bacterium Linked to Painful Stomach Illness," *New York Times*, July 31, 1984, http://www.nytimes.com/1984/07/31/science/new-bacterium-linked-to-painful-stomach-ills.html; Pamela Weintraub, "The Dr. Who Drank Infectious Broth, Gave Himself an Ulcer, and Solved a Medical Mystery," *Discover*, March 2010, http://discovermagazine.com/2010/mar/07-dr-drank-broth-gave-ulcer-solved-medical-mystery.

This attitude toward rules and rule breaking has a name, intelligent disobedience, coined by writer Ira Chaleff, who was first inspired by his observations of how guide dogs are trained to behave at work. Ira Chaleff, *Intelligent Disobedience: Doing Right When What You're Told to Do Is Wrong* (Oakland, CA: Berrett-Koehler, 2015).

Abtin Buergari's story comes from Julie Bort, "This Guy Was Fired and Sued by His Employer, So He Launched a Startup and Got Sweet Revenge," *Business Insider*, April 2014, http://www.businessinsider.com/modus-ceo-from-jobless-to-success-2014-4.

My coverage of Jeffrey Kassing's research into organizational dissent comes from a conversation we had and from Jeffrey Kassing, *Dissent in Organizations* (Cambridge, UK: Polity Press, 2011).

For the USC study on the neurological processes involved in cherished beliefs, see J. T. Kaplan, S. Gimbel, and S. Harris, "Neural Correlates of Maintaining One's Political Beliefs in the Face of Counterevidence," Nature.com, December 23, 2016, https://www.nature.com/articles/srep39589.

Chapter 11

My coverage of Living Room Conversations was informed by my conversations with Joan Blades as well as by Joe Garofoli, "MoveOn Founder, Tea Party Figure Meet," *SFGate*, January 17, 2013, http://www.sfgate.com/politics/joegarofoli/article/MoveOn-founder-Tea-Party-figure-meet-4204384.php#photo-4047180.

Jeffrey Brown's story came to me through direct conversations we had and from Nik DeCosta-Klipa, "How Preachers Cut Violence—by Not Preaching," Boston.com, May 2015, https://www.boston.com/news/local-news/2015/05/31/how-preachers-cut-violence-by-not-preaching; Jeffrey Brown, "How We Cut Youth Violence in Boston by 79 Percent," TED, March 2015, https://www.ted.com/talks/jeffrey_brown_how_we_cut_youth_violence_in_boston_by_79_percent; Lois Beckett, "How the Gun Control Debate Ignores Black Lives," *ProPublica*, November 2015, https://www.propublica.org/article/how-the-gun-control-debate-ignores-black-lives.

Chapter 12

Sources for Helena Foulkes's crusade to end tobacco sales at CVS include Bruce Jaspen, "Why Walgreen Won't Stop Selling Tobacco Like CVS Health," *Forbes*, September 2014, http://www.forbes.com/sites/brucejapsen/2014/09/04/why-walgreen-wont-stop-selling-tobacco-like-cvs-health/#6f167ed2484e; Hiroko Tabuchi, "How CVS Quit Smoking and Grew into a Health Care Giant," *New York Times*, July 12, 2015, http://www.nytimes.com/2015/07/12/business/how-cvs-quit-smoking-and-grew-into-a-health-care-giant.html; Phil Wahba, "The Change Agent Inside CVS," *Fortune*, September 2016, http://fortune.com/2015/09/11/cvs-health-helena-foulkes.

In an exhaustive and widely accepted review of key innovators in art, science, and politics since ancient times, sociologist Randall Collins identified only three who truly acted alone. Randall Collins, *The Sociology of Philosophies: A Global Theory of Intellectual Change* (Cambridge, MA: Harvard University Press, 1998).

The relatively untold story of Stanley Milgram's further experiments into obedience came to me through Ira Chaleff, *Intelligent Disobedience: Doing Right When What You're Told to Do Is Wrong* (Oakland, CA: Berrett-Koehler, 2015).

Over a twenty-month period, University of Richmond's Dejun Tony Kong watched forty-two teams take on a difficult change-management consulting project. He found that not only did the teams made of highly agreeable people perform worse than the more cantankerous teams, but they often couldn't tell things were going wrong. D. T. Kong, L. J. Konczak, and W. P. Bottom, "Team Performance as a Joint Function of Team Member Satisfaction and Agreeableness," *Small Group Research* 46, no. 2 (2015): 160–178, http://journals.sagepub.com/doi/abs/10.1177/1046496414567684.

For the Freakonomics episode on prediction markets, see "Failure Is Your Friend: Full Transcript," Freakonomics, June 4, 2014, http://freakonomics.com/2014/06/04/failure-is-your-friend-full-transcript.

For the pitfalls of and antidotes to shared information bias, see Gwen M. Wittenbaum and Jonathan M. Bowman, "A Social Validation Explanation for Mutual Enhancement," *Journal of Experimental Psychology* 40, no. 2 (March 2004): 169–184, https://scholars.opb.msu.edu/en/publications/a-social-validation-explanation-for-mutual-enhancement-3.

For the study on the effects on creativity of discussing political correctness, see Jack Goncalo et al., "Creativity from Constraint? How Political Correctness Influences Creativity in Mixed-Sex Work Groups," Cornell University, ILR School, August 18, 2014, http://digitalcommons.ilr.cornell.edu/articles/910.

Chapter 13

To tell the story of data falsification in the social sciences, I relied on my conversation with Uri Simonsohn and the following sources: A. Franco, N. Malhotra, and G. Simonovits, "Social Science: Publication Bias in the Social Sciences: Unlocking the File Drawer," *Science* 345, no. 6203 (September 19, 2014): 1502–1505; Joseph P. Simmons, Leif D. Nelson, and Uri Simonsohn, "False-Positive Psychology: Undisclosed Flexibility in Data Collection and Analysis Allows Presenting Anything as Significant," *Psychological Science* 22, no. 11 (October 2011): 1359–1366; Christopher Shea, "The Data Vigilante," *Atlantic*, December 2012, https://www.theatlantic.com/magazine/archive/2012/12/the-data-vigilante/309172.

Epilogue

For the experiment to increase turnout by appealing to the identities of registered voters, see Christopher J. Bryan et al., "Motivating Voter Turnout by Invoking the Self," *Proceedings of the National Academy of Sciences* 108, no. 31 (August 2, 2011): 12653–12656, https://www.ncbi.nlm.nih.gov/pmc/articles/PMC3150938.

INDEX